Back to School

Back to School

Why Everyone Deserves
a Second Chance at Education

MIKE ROSE

THE NEW PRESS

Requests for permission to reproduce selections from this book should be mailed to:
Permissions Department, The New Press, 120 Wall Street, 31st floor, New York, NY 10005.

Originally published in the United States by The New Press, New York, 2012
This paperback edition published by The New Press, 2015
Distributed by Two Rivers Distribution

CIP data is available
ISBN 978-1-59558-786-2 (hc)
ISBN 978-1-59558-803-6 (e-book)
ISBN 978-1-62097-146-8 (pbk)

The New Press publishes books that promote and enrich public discussion
and understanding of the issues vital to our democracy and to a more equitable
world. These books are made possible by the enthusiasm of our readers;
the support of a committed group of donors, large and small;
the collaboration of our many partners in the independent media and
the not-for-profit sector; booksellers, who often hand-sell New Press books;
librarians; and above all by our authors.

www.thenewpress.com

Composition by Bookbright Media
This book was set in Centaur MT

Printed in the United States of America

To those students who are working so hard to create a
second chance for themselves

To the dedicated teachers and tutors, administrators, counselors,
and front-desk staff who keep the door open

And to my parents, Tommy Rose and Rose Meraglio Rose, who
came to the United States as children, their parents seeking a
better life

CONTENTS

Second Chances

THIS IS A BOOK about people in tough circumstances who find their way, who get a second . . . or third . . . or fourth chance, who in some cases feel like they are reinventing themselves. Education can play a powerful role in creating that second chance.

At a time when public institutions are held in low regard and schools at all levels are under assault—for good reasons and bad—*Back to School* demonstrates what education can do, even though it was often earlier schooling that let people down. The stories in this book affirm the transformational potential of the college classroom, the occupational workshop, the tutoring center, the mentoring relationship.

One of the defining characteristics of the United States is its promise of a second chance; this promise is central to our vision of ourselves and to our economic and civic dynamism. When we are at our best as a society, our citizens are not trapped by their histories. Sadly this possibility is shrinking, partly because of a damaged and unstable economy but more so because of our political response to the economy. There are better ways to respond and to foster the growth of a wider sweep of our population. I hope *Back to School* points us in that direction.

Back to School

Why Going Back to School Matters

"YOU MIGHT DISCOVER SOMEBODY you never knew you were," Henry says with a big voice as he turns his wheelchair sideways to look at me. "That's basically what happened to me when I started taking classes here."

Henry is finishing up his requirements—English, sociology—for his associate of arts degree, and he's sending applications to universities across the state. Outside the state as well. His goal is to work in mediation and conflict resolution, particularly with teenagers, kids like he once was, who are "searching for an identity."

Henry is a stocky guy, broad across the chest, with powerful forearms from years in a wheelchair. He wears a baseball cap backward, a sweatshirt—both with the local team's logo—fingerless gloves, baggy shorts, and socks that come up to his knees. His face is vibrant with earnestness.

Henry did well in his first two years of high school, made the honor roll, played football and baseball and wrestled. Then, going into his junior year, he "took a wrong turn" and started "doing young, foolish, dumb stuff." He was caught on campus with marijuana, expelled for a full year, which he spent in an alternative school, came back and graduated on time. "College was the last thing on my mind," he says, so he went to work in a warehouse and got more involved in street life, "running around like a chicken with its head cut off." Two years after graduation, he was arrested for firing a gun into the air during a showdown with a rival gang. He did nineteen months in state prison. "In there all you're known by is your nickname and the gang you're from." He got more of his tattoos—up and down his arms, curving along his neck—while locked up. "When I came out, I went right back to doing the same stupid stuff that got me in trouble." Then "three months to the day" after release, a guy from a rival gang shot him, one bullet hitting his spine, paralyzing him from the waist down. "You're living the fast life, and the next thing you know, your whole world is changed."

The year after the shooting was an "unreal" stream of hospitals and rehab centers, dark thoughts and unsuccessful attempts to stay with his girlfriend. He reports all this without evidence of self-pity or bitterness, but his eyebrows raise in disbelief when he tells me that he went back *once again* to the streets, trying to pick up where he left off. I picture him—for I have seen this over the years—in the midst of four or five guys, swapping stories, big talk, a can of malt liquor cradled in his lap. More of going nowhere.

But his injuries and immobility made him vulnerable to illness, and he was feeling more and more at a loss. Then one day he realized, "You have no place being out on the streets," and that realization eventually led him to go home to his parents' house, a place where people cared about him. "I was in my right mind again." And what he calls his rebirth began.

During those first few months at home, Henry was alone during the day, watching television, surfing the web, thinking about his life. One day, and he's not sure exactly how, he came across information on the community college he now attends. As he read more and more about the college, he knew he had to go, felt an urgency about it, and the next morning, with whatever documents he could lay his hands on, he got on the commuter train "and enrolled right there that day."

Accounts like this are common among the students I've taught and interviewed: a flash of insight, a lightbulb going on, a sudden realization that your life has to change. The insight can hit in the flow of powerful events—a guy lands in jail for the umpteenth time, a loved one leaves you or dies, a seemingly stable job is torn away. It also can come while walking down the street or, as with one young woman, looking out across the retail store where she worked and imagining herself still there in ten years. People say things like "What am I doing?" "Why am I here?" "What's my purpose in life?" "Why did God put me on this earth?"

Henry's paralysis is clearly the life-changing event in his story, but after further time on the streets, and weeks and weeks of being alone with himself, the images of the college on his computer screen called forth a lot of thoughts that catalyzed action: "It's never too late to go back to school." "I just felt like I'm here for a purpose." "It's my turn to give back to my family." "I don't have the use of my legs, but I have the use of my mind."

Henry began by taking occupational courses and earned a certificate as a computer security specialist. But while taking those courses, he got a work-study job as a receptionist at the campus tutoring center, and the experience "opened my eyes." He saw student after student "taking the time out of their day" to get assistance with their papers, wanting to improve their writing. And he saw these other students—the tutors—wanting to help them, working hard to help them. This ongoing flux of the will to improve—seeking help/giving help—must have touched Henry on several levels. His injury certainly led him to appreciate the giving and receiving of assistance. But as well, this interaction provided a huge contrast to the crazy life of the streets, with its brutal rites of dominance, where people do help each other, yes, but within narrow and unforgiving codes of masculinity.

And something else happened. Being around "so many great and positive people who were in the process of transferring" to the university led Henry to discover something else: "That I didn't want to just get an occupational certificate and call it quits. I decided 'I wanna take English courses. I wanna take general education courses.' And that's where it all started for me." There is a strong push these days to create in our schools—K–16—a "college-going culture." Such a culture emerged organically in the small tutoring center of Henry's college, and he is a poster boy for its impact.

I interviewed Henry at a back table of that tutoring center, and I returned to the center later in the day to give him some further information about transferring. Henry and another student were at the computer terminals along the wall opposite the reception desk where he once worked. A tutor was standing slightly behind them, helping both of them, occasionally gesturing toward their screens. I quietly put down my bag and leaned against the desk.

I knew all three. Henry was finishing a thank-you letter to a local civic group that awarded him a small scholarship. The fellow next to him, Jesus, was enrolled in the culinary program and was working on a paper for a Basic English class, a paper I had read earlier on why he's coming back to school. Through his short hair you could still see the thick tattoo on the back of his skull. The tutor, Jeremy, finished his associate's degree at the college and is now close to graduation at a nearby state university. All three had been in prison. And both Jesus and Jeremy had the kind of epiphany Henry describes: Jesus when he found out in prison that he was a father, and Jeremy when, on a whim, he took a class at the college while still in a neighboring halfway house. I imagined these guys on the street four or five years earlier. Depending on what you looked like, the mood they were in, whether they were with their buddies, whether they were high or not, and on what—depending on a lot of things utterly beyond your control—you could find yourself in a nightmare, your life possibly altered as much as Henry's was. One other thing that crossed my mind was that you wouldn't see them pleasantly working together in that little semicircle around the computers. Henry and Jesus are Latino and Jeremy is African American, and there is a tortured, bloody history in this part of the city between Black and Mexican gangs.

By their own accounts, the road they're on is leading Henry, Jesus, and Jeremy to more stable and fulfilling lives than what would have been possible a few years before. This road also has clear payoffs for society: They will climb the income ladder, buying goods and services and paying taxes. Because increased education correlates with a host of extra-economic benefits, they will be more knowledgeable about health and health care, be better able to educate their children, and be more involved in civic affairs. Compared with their previous lives, they will not be adding costs to the criminal justice system, and they will draw on fewer social services. What society had to spend to get them to where they are now—and what it costs to provide their current education—will over time easily provide a significant return on taxpayers' investment.

As we will see, there's a lot wrong with the educational institutions that provide people with a second chance, but this college for these three young men proved to be a place where they could acquire knowledge and skill, develop a sense of competence as readers and writers and thinkers, channel desire into productive activity, come to terms with inner and outer demons, bridge social divides, take on a new way of being in the world. To be sure, I'm talking about a small percentage of all those on the streets or in the criminal justice system. And by no means do all who try to return to school stay more than a few weeks or months. But when it happens, it broadens our vision of the possible. As Henry said, "You might discover somebody you never knew you were."

Throughout the pages of this book, you will meet people who, like Henry, Jesus, and Jeremy, are using one of our society's postsecondary or adult-education institutions to redirect their lives in ways that benefit both them and society. In some cases they have been through the criminal justice system. Much more often, they are nonoffenders who for a mix of personal and institutional reasons didn't do so well in school. You'll meet people who had terrible, chaotic childhoods that made success in anything difficult. You'll meet people for whom things went fairly smoothly—in school and out—but who moved straight into the workforce after high school to help support their parents and siblings or to start families of their own. And there are people whose lives were suddenly turned upside down by divorce, illness, or death. There are veterans who can't find work and workers who lost jobs they held for years. Some are young; some are much older. They are White and non-White, urban and rural. Some come from families that have been in the United States—even in the same community—for generations, and some are new to this country, repeating a pattern of immigration that goes back to the early days of the Republic. In other words, you'll meet a wide cross-section of America.

Recently, a flurry of books has been written by university presidents and faculty, by educational researchers, and by longtime observers of college life about the sorry state of higher education in the United States. Collectively, these books list a number of legitimate concerns: from skyrocketing tuition and the incoherence of the lower-division curriculum to the production of trivial research and the reliance on adjunct faculty. What is telling is that almost all of these books—I'm familiar with fifteen, and there are more—deal with research universities and elite colleges and focus on the traditional undergraduate fresh out of high school and entering college at eighteen or nineteen, headed for a bachelor's degree.

Only a few books include state colleges or community colleges in their analyses. None mentions alternative pathways that for some lead to college, like the General Educational Development Test or GED. Yet, increasingly, postsecondary students in the United States are not coming to college out of high school, they are not attending full-time, and they are absolutely not eighteen or nineteen. Here are two telling statistics: the number of single parents among undergraduates has nearly doubled in the last twenty years, and since 1970 the percentage of undergraduates over forty has more than doubled. The "nontraditional" student is becoming the norm. So it is in the thousands of state universities and local four-year and two-year colleges across the country where hugely important stories about postsecondary education are being played out.

In fact, one could argue that our nation's economic and civic future lies more in the health of these institutions than in the schools that regularly end up in the *U.S. News and World Report*'s annual listing of the top fifty colleges and universities. I'm not trying to dim the luster of this top fifty—the aforementioned critiques of U.S. higher education already do that—but rather to underscore the fact that most education beyond high school in the United States goes on elsewhere.

To be sure, the schools and programs that are the focus of *Back to School* also serve the children of well-to-do families: these students go to a community college, for example, to save money that, upon transfer to a university, can be used to fund further education beyond the bachelor's degree. And both community colleges and adult schools offer a variety of courses taken for enrichment by a broad range of the community.

But the majority of the more than 10 million students in community colleges, and especially in adult school academic and occupational programs, are from low- to modest-income backgrounds. And some live in poverty. For the most part, they have not benefited from high-performing schools or quality educational resources. They typically must work—some full-time or close to it—have family obligations, and have limited transportation. The schools and programs they attend provide the primary, if not only, avenue for them to further their education. This is particularly true in rural America. As a steady stream of reports on the American economy from federal, state, and private agencies have claimed, both workforce development as well as attainment of bachelor's and graduate degrees will stagnate without the achievement of this large and varied population.

It is in these institutions that we can get a measure of how we're doing as a society on a number of questions that are fundamental to our best sense of who we are. How well are we preparing students from a broad sweep of backgrounds for life after high school, and how adequate are the programs we have in place to remedy the failures of K–12 education? How robust is our belief in the ability of the common person, and what opportunities do we provide to realize that ability? Given the nature of Western capitalism, what mechanisms are there to compensate for boom and bust economic cycles, for "creative destruction," for globalization? Do we have an adequate social safety net, and how effective are we at providing people a second chance? How open and welcoming are our core institutions—such as postsecondary education—and how adaptable?

The problem is that these second-chance institutions are not living up to their promise, and the current political climate poses threats to their improvement and, in some cases, to their continued existence.

———————

Community college graduation rates offer one indicator of the limited effectiveness of our second-chance institutions. The majority of students entering community college say they want to graduate, but only about 30 percent complete a degree or credential or transfer within four years. There are a number of reasons offered for these disappointing results.

For all the diverse talents and strengths those entering the community college system bring to it, many students have a lot to overcome, ranging from poor educations and family disruptions to unstable employment, housing, and health care. They have not been on the educational fast track and don't come from families with much experience in higher education, so they aren't that familiar with institutional policies and norms. For older students, there's the additional burden of not having been in a classroom in decades. "I hated school," one woman told me, "and to be back in it is really strange." Some students, younger ones particularly, come because they know it will help them get a better job or because parents urge it or friends are going, but they don't have a particular goal in mind, which, combined with a lack of institutional savvy, leads to low levels of engagement, unfocused course selection, and sporadic attendance.

What is significant, though, is that some community colleges get better results than others with students who share similar background characteristics. Demography affects but does not determine achievement; what the college does matters. I will have more to say about this in upcoming chapters, but let me here sketch the institutional barriers to student success. We find some of these barriers in the full range of postsecondary institutions, community college to Ivy League university, but they are especially vexing for the typical community college student who has fewer resources to overcome them.

At the policy and administrative level, many colleges—especially those in large higher ed systems—are hard to navigate: Guidelines and requirements for matriculation, financial aid, or transfer are complicated by decades of independently made policy decisions that lack coherence. Counseling staff are overloaded (on some campuses a single counselor can be responsible for two thousand students). And different levels and kinds of advising (from an academic department, from the financial aid office, from the transfer center) can be fragmented, leading to contradictory advice. Even after spending a year or two at some colleges, I have a hard time wrapping my head around the many options and requirements involved in remedial courses in math, writing, and reading.

When it comes to curriculum and teaching, course sequences and requirements can be confusing. Here's a small but telling example: It's not uncommon that the three sequenced remedial writing courses leading to transfer-level English will have non-sequential, seemingly random numbers such as English 68, 25, and 30. The same holds true for reading and for math. Of more concern, little coordinated thought is typically given to how to address the limited skills and background knowledge of many of the students wanting to take academic or occupational courses. As for faculty, one finds—as in any profession—a wide range of competence and commitment, from people going through the motions to exceptionally gifted teachers deeply committed to their students. But community college teaching loads are daunting, and, increasingly, courses are taught by adjunct faculty holding down jobs on two or three campuses. So mounting a coordinated response to student need is difficult at best. As one instructor at a midwestern college put it, "It's hard to get the conversation going when we're all teaching five sections of writing."

Then there is the complex web of traditions, turf and status dynamics, and beliefs about institutional mission, the purpose of education, and the abilities of the student population. These symbolic and ideological issues emerge when you probe administrative structures or curriculum or staff and faculty behavior, and, to my mind, they represent the most formidable barriers to change. Some examples: The long-standing tension between the academic and the vocational mission of the community college, the deep-rooted erroneous beliefs about learning that shape most remedial programs, the very different, frequently not articulated, philosophies of education held by staff and faculty.

On the campuses that are more successful, various combinations of enterprising faculty, department chairs and program directors, mid-level managers and top brass—though not always all these actors—are able to coordinate services and provide more structure and guidance for entering students, revise or create curricula that more directly address student needs, and develop ways to work through administrative and ideological tangles.

I want to return to those dreary statistics about student success. Though there is wide agreement that our second-chance institutions (and postsecondary institutions in general) have to do better, some of us are also concerned that these aggregated rates of completion of degrees and rates of transfer don't reflect the multiple reasons why people go to a community college—and why they leave. Even though the majority of students upon entry do say they want to complete a certificate or degree, many, in fact, shift to shorter-term goals, in some instances because of inadequacies in a college's services and curriculum, but also in response to personal needs, family demands, or opportunities in the job market.

One young man, a high school dropout with past addiction problems, entered an electrical construction program and over his first year got absorbed in school, developed some literacy and numeracy and trade skills, and began to see himself in a different light. He quit before completing the occupational certificate to join the navy where he could continue his education, clear his debts, and have a potential career before him. A woman with two kids already had a low-level job in the fashion industry, and she entered a fashion program to take four or five courses that built sufficient skills to get a better job in her company. Both of these people would be recorded as dropouts, a failure both for them and their college. It is also the case that approximately

60 percent of community college students attend more than one community college, so we won't get a complete picture of their postsecondary experience by focusing on their exit from the initial college.

There are efforts, therefore, to develop more discrete indicators of student progress and college effectiveness. How many students complete their remedial requirements within a certain time frame, or transfer-level English or math, or thirty units—a number associated with labor market payoffs? These and other benchmarks correlate with student success, and they give a better indication of how well a college is doing its job. And, significantly, these more discrete measures can be used by an institution to create strategic counseling and instructional interventions, such as zeroing in on transfer-level math.

It is characteristic of our time to rely heavily on statistical measures in forming public policy; we count, and calculate averages and ratios, seeking clarity in numbers. I appreciate the value of statistical analysis and use it in my own work. But such analysis, especially the fairly broad kind used in policy making—tallies, percentages, trends—fills in only part of the picture of complex human reality. Some studies do combine interviews and other on-the-ground information with analysis of numerical data, but such studies are rare. The typical study would not capture the motives and decisions of that woman in the fashion program and the guy who joined the navy. Furthermore, no matter how refined the collection and analysis of statistical data, without knowledge of the history and culture and daily reality of the place from which the data were collected, policy makers can make huge blunders, as the history of failures in urban renewal and agricultural development illustrate. In general, the makers of education policy have not learned this lesson.

The heightened attention these studies of student success have brought to the community college (and likewise to adult school) has definitely put reform of two-year colleges on the map—a welcome development, for that segment of postsecondary education typically gets little attention. Federal and state governments and private foundations have sponsored initiatives aimed at increasing student success, and the many people within colleges who for some time have been pushing for improvements have received a welcome boost.

The issue I just mentioned about the need for intimate knowledge of institutions comes into play here. These initiatives naturally are geared toward results, more students hitting those aforementioned benchmarks and end goals. The ensuing pressure and accountability might jolt those campuses paralyzed by ossified traditions, infighting, and inertia. That would be a blessing. But we have to be careful about the mechanisms we put in place, for—as recent No Child Left Behind–driven K–12 reform has demonstrated—the fix can lead to unintended negative consequences. For example, there are proposals—and some attempts—to tie funding to these benchmarks: budgets will be affected by the percentage of students that exit remediation or gain those thirty units or complete a certificate or degree. This has a common-sense appeal, but one predictable result will be for formerly open-access colleges to put a floor on whom they admit, accepting only those who have a better chance of succeeding, limiting opportunity for the most vulnerable. (Henry, the fellow in the wheelchair, had scores on his initial English placement test low enough to have denied him admission in this more restrictive environment.) Or small programs that are successful will be pressured to expand, to be brought to scale before they're ready or in a way that replicates the superficial features of the program but loses its heart, the qualities that make it work.

There is one other thing that worries me about the current reform environment. The continual broadcasting of high failure rates—statistics that, as I've been suggesting, might not tell the full story—can, over time, breed a sense of hopelessness in the public and lead policy makers to cut funds or redirect them. I've been watching, and have written about, this kind of thing happening in K–12 education. The headlines on the newspaper articles reporting on these studies of failure crystallize my concern: "Billions Spent in U.S. on Community College Students Who Drop Out," or "Failing Students Get Federal Aid." That sort of message can spark action, but it also leads to backlash and withdrawal of support.

The challenge as I see it is to be clear-eyed and vigilant about the performance of our second-chance institutions but to use methods of investigation that capture a fuller story of the institutions and the people in them. As well, we need to find, study, and broadcast the many examples of successful work being done daily in these places and build our analysis and our solutions on illustrations of the possible.

America loves the underdog, the come-from-behind winner, the tale of personal redemption, the rags-to-riches story. In *Ragged Dick*, Horatio Alger's novel about an enterprising boot-black, one of the author's fictitious benefactors offers the following rosy observation about upward mobility in the United States: "In this free country poverty is no bar to a man's advancement." The belief that individual effort can override social circumstances runs deep in the national psyche. It's in Ben Franklin's writing, it's in Alger's immensely popular nineteenth-century novels, and it is a central tenet in conservative social policy today.

How noteworthy it is then that a recent issue of the influential conservative magazine *National Review* posed this question in bold print on its cover: *What's Wrong with Horatio Alger?* Above the question, the young Alger protagonist sits forlorn on a park bench, his shoeshine kit unused, an untied bundle of newspapers next to him, unsold. The standard political discourse from the Right contains no such question. The party line is that the market, if left alone, will produce the opportunity for people to advance, that the current sour economy—though worrisome and painful—will correct itself if commerce and innovation are allowed to thrive, and that the gap between rich and poor is, in itself, not a sign of any basic malfunction or injustice, for there are always income disparities in capitalism. For government to draw on the money some citizens have earned to assist those who are less fortunate is to interfere with market principles, dampen the raw energy of capitalism, and foster dependency. The opportunity to advance up the ladder of mobility is always there for those who work hard. This is a seamless story, made plausible by our deep belief in upward mobility.

But the author of the lead article in *National Review* cites statistics that pretty much all economists across the ideological spectrum confirm: Upward mobility for people at the bottom rungs of the income ladder, limited during the best of times, is significantly diminished. Breaking the numbers out by race the author writes of "a national tragedy," that "Black and White children grow up in entirely different economic worlds." "Living up to our values," the writer suggests, "requires policymakers . . . to focus on increasing upward relative mobility from the bottom."

The *Economist*, not as fiscally conservative as *National Review*, but in the same free-market ballpark, put it even more strongly in another recent cover story. The writers say that the real danger to the American economy is chronic, ingrained joblessness that is related to our social and economic structure: tens of millions of young, marginally educated people who drift in and out of low-paying, dead-end jobs and older low-skilled displaced workers, unable to find employment as industries transform and jobs disappear. This situation places a huge and, if left alone, intractable drag on the economy. Therefore, the editors recommend comprehensive occupational, educational, and social services, for America spends "much less as a share of GDP than almost any other rich country" on policies to get the hard-to-employ into the labor market.

This is the context in which we are considering our second-chance institutions. Many of the people we're discussing are facing hardships beyond what education alone can remedy, including inadequate housing, health care, child care, and, ultimately, employment—just a decent wage and a few benefits. But for some, improving English or math or gaining a GED certificate or an occupational skill or a postsecondary degree would contribute to their economic stability.

Yet, right at the point when they are most needed, our second-chance institutions are being threatened with severe budget cuts. Across the country, community colleges, adult schools, and literacy programs are reporting record enrollments at the same time they have to trim staff, classes, and services. A number of colleges can offer only a smattering of courses in the summer. Nationwide, hundreds of thousands of people are on waiting lists or simply denied admission. On the other side of this coin are rural and semirural institutions that have lost enrollment over the years because of changing demographic patterns. They are facing closure, even though for those still in the community, they are the only resource of their kind available. One more thing: The public library—an iconic American institution—is reducing hours and staff and closing local branches. And this is at a time when two-thirds of the nation's libraries provide the only free Internet access in their communities—and when government and employment information and forms are increasingly going online.

The immediate cause of these cuts is the terrible recession beginning in 2008. Policy makers face "unprecedented challenges" and "have no other choice" but to make cuts in education. Doing more with less has become, in the words of Secretary of Education Arne Duncan, "the new normal." The word *austerity* has entered our national conversation with a vengeance. As I write this, the Los Angeles Unified School District is considering eliminating its entire adult education program, twenty-four community schools, serving over 250,000 people.

I don't dispute the immense difficulty of budgeting in a recession nor the fact that education spending includes waste that should be eliminated. But when our situation is represented as inevitable and normal, the recession becomes a catastrophe without culpability. The civic and moral dimension of both the causes of the recession and the way policy makers respond to it is neutralized.

What is especially worthy of scrutiny is the role right-wing economic ideology is playing in these policy deliberations—and as the economy improves, the Right's beliefs will still be a potent force in public policy. Antigovernment, anti–welfare state, antitax, this ideology forcefully undercuts broadscale public responses to hardship. Such responses are tarred as a "redistribution of wealth," moving money, as Rep. Paul Ryan puts it, from the "makers" to the "takers." Decisions are made on a ledger sheet profoundly bounded by simplistic assumptions about economics and opportunity and naive, often bigoted, beliefs about people who need help.

For the most part, conservatives support the idea of second-chance educational and training programs, but many would insist that the programs trim their costs and slash the financial aid that enables students to attend them. These policy makers also resist the kinds of services that many students need to continue their education: health and child care, rehabilitation programs, housing. So they support the idea of a second chance while undercutting most of what makes a second chance possible.

Equal opportunity is something every conservative affirms as a core American value. Yet in no realistic sense of the word does anything like equal opportunity exist toward the bottom of the income ladder. And some argue that opportunity exist is eroding toward the middle as well. Recent studies show that parental income has a greater effect on children's success in America than in other developed countries. A report from the Pell Institute, for example, shows an astonishing 47 percent gap in the attainment of bachelor's degrees between young people at the top half versus bottom half of our country's income distribution. As that writer in *National Review* noted, low-income children live in a different economic world.

Many of the students I've taught at UCLA who come from well-to-do families grew up in a world of museums, music lessons, tutoring, sports programs, travel, up-to-date educational technologies, after-school and summer programs geared toward the arts or sciences. All this is a supplement to attending good to exceptional public or private schools. Because their parents are educated, they can provide all kinds of assistance with homework, with navigating school, with advocacy. These parents are doing everything possible to create maximum opportunity for their kids, often with considerable anxiety and expense. There's no faulting them; poor parents would do the same if they could. But it would require quite a distortion to see young people from affluent and poor backgrounds as having an equal opportunity at academic and career success. To legitimize their view of the economy and society, then, conservatives have to justify advantage.

One way to account for unequal opportunity is to claim that intelligence is a factor and that the families and their children at the lower end of things are there because they're not that bright—so various compensatory programs, in fact, won't help that much. You'll certainly hear this kind of talk in private, and a few bold pundits like Charles Murray, of *The Bell Curve* fame, say it in public. But scientifically it doesn't hold water, and it is so politically unpalatable that few politicians would risk uttering it. In various ways, a number of the chapters in *Back to School* address this issue of social class and intelligence.

Another way to explain away inequality—one that has a long history in the United States and is still very much with us—is the moral argument. People are at the lower end of the economy because of a failure of character; they engage in counterproductive behavior, lack a work ethic, don't complete things, and so on. They are a drain on the system, gaming it, on the dole. Since Ronald Reagan's infamous "welfare queen" invocation, conservative political discourse has been brimming with such imagery, as the 2012 GOP primaries demonstrated. There is both a theory of the social order and good, old-fashioned prejudice at play here—and both are enhanced by the social isolation of the rich from the poor.

I don't want to minimize the deep philosophical differences between the conservative and liberal perspectives on social issues, but I do think that some conservatives would be surprised to see first-hand the work ethic, the lack of excuses for previous bad behavior and blunders, the self-reliance, multiple responsibilities, and schedules of the people who populate this book.

I've been working with one group of students who begin classes at 7:00 A.M., then work, participate in student government, go to the library to study, and leave in the evening—usually by public transportation—to homes that are anything but stable (thus the refuge of the library). One young man is currently homeless, sleeping in his inoperable car parked at a friend's family's house. He's at school every day by 6:00 A.M. to clean up and get his day in order.

Of course there are people at their school who are drifting, drawing what resources they can, sometimes deluding themselves, sometimes consciously gaming the system. I'll have more to say about this later, but for now let me note that the students I'm mentoring can point them out in a heartbeat—because they are not the norm. Furthermore, and it's a sign of the times that I even have to write this, such behaviors appear across the socioeconomic landscape. The deplorable thing is the degree to which moral and character flaws are disproportionately attributed to poor people. But if you are able to penetrate the ideological fog and actually enter other people's lives, you'll witness a quite different and much more complex human reality.

Finally, the Right justifies advantage by defining opportunity as an individual phenomenon and representing obstacles to mobility as clear and local and within one's personal power to overcome. This definition yields a particular version of the rags to riches story, which takes us back to the young Horatio Alger character sitting on that park bench. Conservatives use rise-from-hardship narratives to great effect, for the narratives confirm their claims about the ever-presence of opportunity, regardless of background. But one of the most striking things about conservative celebrations of social mobility is that they are accounts of hardship with almost no *feel* of hardship to them. They reflect a kind of opportunity that exists only in fiction. Obstacles receive brief mention—if they're mentioned at all—and anger, doubt, or despair are virtually absent. You won't see the home health care worker whose back is a wreck or the guys at bitter loose ends when the factory closes. You won't see people, exhausted, shuttling between two or more jobs to make a living or the anxious scramble for minimal health care for their kids.

The Right's stories present a world stripped of the physical and moral insult of poverty. Characters move upward, driven by self-reliance, optimism, faith, responsibility. Though there might be an occasional reference to teachers or employers who were impressed with the candidate's qualities, the explanations for the candidate's achievements rest pretty much within his or her individual spirit. The one exception is parents: They are usually mentioned as the source of virtue. Family values as the core of economic mobility.

In the Alger originals, the lucky break, the fortuitous encounter is key to the enterprising hero's ascent. Alger's narrator states: "Not many boys can expect an uninterrupted course of prosperity when thrown upon their own exertions." It's worth dwelling on this sentence, for there's little play of chance and good fortune in the contemporary conservative version. Luck's got nothing to do with it. And you surely will not hear a whisper about legislation or social movements that may have enhanced opportunity, opened a door, or removed an obstacle. It would be hard to find a more radically individual portrait of achievement.

The stories of mobility that I know differ greatly from the conservative script. To be sure, there is hard work and perseverance and faith—sometimes deeply religious faith. But many people with these same characteristics don't make it out of poverty. Discrimination is intractable, or the local economy is devastated to the core, or the consequences of poor education cannot be overcome, or one's health gives out, or family ties (and, often, tragedy) overwhelm.

The people who do succeed—and their gains are typically modest—often tell stories of success mixed with setbacks, of two steps forward and one back. Such stories reveal anger and nagging worry or compromise and ambivalence or a bruising confrontation with one's real or imagined inadequacies—"falling down within me," as one woman in an adult literacy program put it. This is the lived experience of social class. No wonder that these truer stories typically give great significance to help of some kind, both private and public. A relative, a friend, or a minister lends a hand. Family and community social networks open up an opportunity. A local occupational center provides training. The government's safety net—food stamps and welfare, Medicaid, and public housing—protects one from devastation.

It is, then, a tight bundle of reductive economic and social theory, a fanciful definition of opportunity, and negative beliefs about the poor that have become such a force in truly difficult budget negotiations, and there does not seem to be an equally powerful economic *and* moral counter-voice in those deliberations to check it.

———————

As the editors of the *Economist* pointed out, the United States does not currently have robust policies to help low-income people enter and thrive in the labor market. Among the few policy initiatives in place are ones aimed at increasing enrollments in postsecondary education, and several private foundations, notably Gates and Lumina, have been sponsoring such initiatives as well. These efforts are laudable; however, they reach a fairly small percentage of poor and low-income Americans and on average are targeted toward the more academically skilled among them—though many still require remedial English and mathematics.

The economic rationale for increased postsecondary education rests on some widely held—and continually broadcasted—assumptions. Work in the "new economy" requires more literacy, numeracy, and computer skills as well as so-called "soft skills" like collaboration and communication. A further assumption is that there is a "skills mismatch" between many Americans and the labor market; that is, there are jobs out there that go unfilled because the local labor pool doesn't possess the technological or behavioral skills to do the work. These beliefs have become gospel, repeated daily in policy speeches and documents and on opinion pages. And they do fuel enrollments in adult schools, colleges, and private occupational schools. There is some truth in them. A lot of the jobs that were available to someone with limited education in the mid-twentieth century have been automated and outsourced. And some specialized businesses across the country can't readily get the kind of employee they need. But the *overall* economic picture is more complicated.

First of all, in many sectors of the labor market, there are simply fewer jobs to be had because of changes in technology and the way work is organized. And Americans are working longer and harder, creating increases in production but not in jobs or salaries. Many jobs, both blue-collar and white, are also being broken down into components and outsourced. Your service representative is speaking to you from India or the Philippines. The traditional correlation between increased education and income still holds, but a whole lot of people with bachelor's degrees and beyond are out of work or working at a job that requires no college degree at all.

A particularly trenchant critique of the standard line on education and jobs is offered by political economist Gordon Lafer who argues that the fundamental problem with the economy is the shortage of jobs and the absence of vigorous job creation policies. It is a political "charade," as he puts it, to push job training as the solution to unemployment, for this approach shifts the blame for unemployment and income inequality onto workers themselves, onto their lack of "higher-order thinking skills," or "soft skills," or the "mismatch" between their skills and the skills that industry demands. In fact, the jobs aren't there, and short-term training in job-seeking strategies or basic skills does not make an appreciable difference in helping people get the limited number of jobs that do exist.

Lafer is targeting a particular set of policies and training programs primarily connected to the Workforce Investment Act, not necessarily the kinds of educational experiences I'm concerned with in this book, though there can be some overlap. But the larger point he makes is important here, for there is in the air the belief that education itself will lift people out of hard times. So let me be clear. I am not claiming that the education provided by second-chance institutions alone will guarantee mobility, be an economic magic bullet. I agree wholeheartedly with the call for better economic policy, for I see what happens when people work hard, build skills, gain a certificate or degree, and then go out into a world with no jobs or apprenticeships. It is indeed a cruel charade.

I am championing second-chance programs because I believe that when well executed they develop skills and build knowledge that can lead to employment but also provide a number of other personal, social, and civic benefits. There is an economic rationale for championing these programs—and these days the economic rationale is the only one that has a prayer of swaying policy makers—but school is about more than a paycheck.

To my mind, education and job creation are not an either/or proposition. There is a political battle over employment to be waged. And there is work to be done in the classroom. And at times the two come together. Students meet others in similar circumstances and broaden their understanding of their own hardships. They are exposed to economics, political science, history that, I'll be the first to admit, can simply be another bunch of stuff to memorize and get out of the way but also can provide perspectives on society and one's place in it. This is where good teaching is so important. Some students join clubs, trade organizations, or student government or get jobs on campus, all of which can provide the occasion to develop social networks and be exposed to new activities and bodies of knowledge. And as students become more literate and numerate, as they develop their interests or acquire new ones, as they learn trade skills, as they feel their minds working, this all affects the way they move through the world and act on it. One study suggests that nearly 20 percent of community college students decide to pursue further education after enrolling in their two-year institution. To the degree that educational programs and job creation are in conflict, it is solely because of political manipulation and not because the two are naturally antagonistic.

I believe deeply in what schooling can accomplish. And part of our problem—on the right and the left—has been that for decades we have reduced school, K–16, to an economic institution. But it is more than that, and throughout our history we have affirmed that education—for children and for adults, in the schoolhouse and in self-improvement associations—yields multiple benefits to self and society. I think back to those three guys—Henry, Jesus, and Jeremy—at the computer terminals talking about writing. So much happened during their years at the college that led to that moment; so many kinds of learning made that moment possible. To be sure, their work at the computers had an economic purpose to it, and it might even be possible to estimate in some crude way the economic payoff. But if that's all you're looking for, then you'll miss most of what is valuable to them and to the world beyond them.

There are a number of means by which people can get a second chance in the United States: through education, through churches and faith-based institutions, through government programs and the military, through civic and community-based organizations, through labor unions, and through a wide range of private business and philanthropic initiatives. I'm focusing on education, and particularly on the community college and, to a lesser degree, the adult school. I refer to literacy programs, but did not have access to a substantial one during the writing of this book, although I have in the past and will draw on that experience. In addition to libraries, community organizations, and churches, adult literacy instruction is also found in adult schools and some community colleges, so we will meet men and women along the way who are trying to learn to read and write.

Private occupational colleges—often called proprietary schools—have been in existence since the late nineteenth century (correspondence schools were one early example), and they have been undergoing a boom in the last few decades. They focus on specific job training, from fashion and culinary to engineering. As with any institution—particularly a rapidly growing one—there is a range of quality in proprietary schools, from ones that are well established and accredited to those that have been the subject of criminal investigation for fraud. Proprietary schools are not represented in *Back to School*, for I want to focus on institutions that have a broader educational mission; even though community colleges and adult schools do offer occupational training (and we will witness a lot of it), that training, at least in theory, is embedded in a more educationally comprehensive institutional philosophy. I am also focusing on the public domain, on institutions that the society sees as worth supporting as part of the public good, as integral to the development of its citizens. This is a book about the public, as well as personal, meaning of a second chance.

ONE

Adult Education and the Landscape of Opportunity

"As you can hear from my accent," the coordinator says as she distributes flyers to the women and men seated at the tables before her, "I came from another country, too." The fifteen people at the tables are in an advanced English as a Second Language class, and some of them will be moving on to the district's Adult Basic Education program where a smaller number will further transition into the coordinator's GED classes to eventually earn a high school equivalency certificate. It will be a long journey.

"I was an ESL student like you," the coordinator continues, "I sat in these chairs many years ago." Behind her projected on the white board is a list of the GED subject areas:

Language Arts – Reading
Language Arts – Writing
Mathematics
Social Studies
Science

"Now I am teaching the classes I took. So be patient. You will achieve your goals."

In the audience are three men: one Ethiopian, two Filipino. Two women are from the Middle East. The rest, all women, are Chinese and Korean. Most of the students are in their twenties. As the coordinator is explaining Adult Basic Education and the GED program, a number of the students are nodding and softly voicing the signals of comprehension, *uh huh, mmm. . . .* Their ESL course, after all, is focused on speaking and listening. When the coordinator tells her personal story, the murmur of understanding increases in tempo. A young Korean woman in a purple jacket, feathery fringe around the collar, leans forward: the lead in the chorus.

The ESL program is located in an old building along the perimeter of one of the district's middle schools, not far from the adult school offices and classrooms. On the drive back, the coordinator, Maria, explains a little about the ESL population. Some have done well in the equivalent of high school in their home country. They are fully literate in their native language and know math and science. A few, like her, might have postsecondary degrees—Maria's is in physical geography—and they will do very well here as their English improves.

Other students had to work or had children early, or were restricted by cultural norms, or were caught up in political turmoil or war, so their education was disrupted, sometimes at an early age. As Maria drives, she leans forward slightly, intent on the road but fluid in conversation, tapping the fingers of her right hand on the steering wheel to punctuate what she's been telling me. These students, the ones whose schooling was cut short, have years of study in front of them, but, if—a big *if*, Maria acknowledges—

employment and family arrangements work out, they'll make it. They will make it. She tells me that I will see some of last semester's ESL cohort in the basic education class in the building that comes into view as we round the corner into the parking lot of the adult school.

—————

There are a little over four thousand adult education programs in the United States. They vary state by state, but the typical offerings include general enrichment classes (cooking and crafts, fitness, computers, local history and geography) and the kinds of classes that concern us here: occupational education and job training, English as a Second Language, Adult Basic Education (typically for people with elementary literacy and mathematics skills), and Adult Secondary Education—typically as preparation for the GED or the high school diploma itself. Maria coordinates Adult Secondary Education in her district. In some states, adult education is organizationally housed within K–12; in others it's connected to postsecondary education, particularly the community college system; and in yet other states it's aligned with both K–12 and postsecondary education. It's a complex mosaic nationwide, but the important thing to note for our purposes is that the particular arrangement has consequences for budgets and for the kinds of programs that can be developed. At a community college in the Midwest that I visited, for example, GED instruction blends with the college's health sciences curriculum, leading students not only to GED completion, but also to course work for an occupational certificate or an associate's degree.

Maria leaves me at the Basic Education classroom and goes down to her office to prepare for her math class. The room is about fifteen feet wide and thirty feet long with off-white walls, and a mix of natural and muted fluorescent light resulting in a soft, clean illumination. Bookcases, filing cabinets, and small stands and tables line the four walls; maps and posters are arranged symmetrically between and above them. The teacher, Kevin, a lean, long-haired, affable guy admits with an apologetic forward shrug of the shoulders that he's "a neat freak." The books, and there are many of them, are mostly workbooks and reference books geared toward the middle grades (*Reading Power, Breakthroughs in Math, Grammar in Context*), dictionaries, encyclopedias, and abridged fiction: Jack London, Kate Chopin, Richard Wright. The room is orderly but inviting. On the teacher's desk is a small vase of blue and yellow papier-mâché flowers. By the door hangs a skeleton, about three-quarters human scale, a pair of Groucho glasses with black bushy eyebrows resting on the skull's bony ridge.

Students sit in three general areas of the room: at two rectangular tables in the center before the main whiteboard; at another rectangular table off to the left, facing a whiteboard on the west wall; and, on the other side of the room, at an oval table where one-on-one tutoring takes place. A teacher and several aides—most of the aides are volunteers—provide both small group and individual instruction. On the day Maria drops me off, eleven students sit at the central tables with Kevin, the teacher, and seven sit at the table to the left with an aide who is a retired engineer. Two students receive individual instruction in basic reading

("Which of these words begins with an 'M' sound?") at the oval table.

The curriculum is a traditional one. Today both the main table and table to the left are doing a series of vocabulary-building exercises, although the level of difficulty is different. During the hour, students match words (*morale, colleague, gauge*) with definitions, then they write sentences containing the words, which the teacher dictates: "My colleague who designed the computer program is responsible for its success." The students then write the dictated sentences on the board and, as a group, decide whether a sentence has an error and, if so, edit it. I suspect that the majority of Adult Basic Education programs around the country use a language arts curriculum similar to this one, although some programs draw more on creative-writing assignments or on local history and the life experiences of the participants or on employment-related topics and materials.

Most of the students in the room are in their twenties and thirties; several are older, and there is a sharply dressed woman in her sixties who, the teacher tells me, comes for the social contact, to improve her English, and, in her own words, "to keep my mind alert." Five of the twenty students are native speakers of English, one of whom is a man with a first- or second-grade reading level. Most students are Latino or African American, two are Filipino, and one young woman is from Poland. Some have recently transitioned from ESL, but most have been in the United States for some time and are now at a place in their lives when they can come back to school. Most are here to improve their English, and, as the teacher puts it, they all have a goal: in some cases, they had a job and built skills but got laid off and want to improve their English to get another job. Some want to go all the way through to earning the GED certificate. The counselor, Betty, tells me of a woman who, due to child care and work, could come for only one hour per day but did so for years and eventually took and passed the GED exam. In other parts of the country, the ethnic and racial composition would be different, but the kinds of stories would be the same. As Betty puts it, these are people who are trying to change their lives.

The class seems engaged and the students interact easily— some on the shy side, some outgoing—with the instructor and with each other. In some sense their participation matches the feel of the room. Interaction is orderly, structured by the nature of the curriculum—workbook exercises, questions and answers, dictation and response—but not rigidly so. The instructors have a nice way about them, their voices—from baritone to tenor— have a pleasant modulation, encouraging, respectfully upbeat. And although the discussion is focused, there is ample room for digression. The vocabulary word *autobiography* leads Kevin to ask what famous autobiography wasn't actually an autobiography? (*The Autobiography of Malcolm X*, which was written by Alex Haley). To the side I hear an aide follow up on a question about biography versus fiction and explain the genre of historical fiction. The word *amateur* leads another aide to acknowledge that one of the Latina students speaks French. And a student's comment about a radio spot on chewing gum as enhancing test taking leads Kevin to speculate with the class as to how they might set up an experiment to test that claim.

I slide my chair over toward the oval table to better hear Jennifer, the aide working with the student on basic reading. He is an African American man in his mid-forties, broad chested, dressed neatly but in well-worn shirt and trousers. "Last week I went to a class on job safety," he reads slowly as Jennifer helps him. They have been working on this material for a while, and he moves through it with a firm voice. Jennifer tells me that his posture at the desk has gotten straighter over the last few months. He grew up in the rural Midwest, barely went to school, has lived off of basic labor, recently came out of prison, and is determined to learn to read. Though he is still learning to match letters and combinations of letters to sounds, his printing of those letters is perfect. He has wanted to learn to read and write for a long time, and perfecting his script was one thing he could do. You'll find students like him in Adult Basic Education, but more often in adult literacy programs in libraries, churches, or community-based organizations. In this relatively small district, though, there are few such programs, and none offered through the library. So he started coming to Kevin's class.

I am struck by the diversity of backgrounds and skills in this single room. People with postsecondary degrees from another country and a man who has barely been inside a schoolhouse. People in their early twenties, a lifetime in front of them, and a woman with grandchildren, who comes to school to keep her mind alert. People navigating cultures and languages. People starting over. One of the things he particularly enjoys about the place, Kevin tells me, is seeing an eighteen-year-old African American kid who grew up down the street forming friendships around a common goal with a forty-five-year-old mother from Central America or the Philippines or Southeast Asia. There aren't many places where that can happen.

———————

"No one can hide from her," was one of the first things I heard about Maria, and it was meant as a big compliment. She is in her late forties, of medium height, shoulder-length brown hair cut in a simple style. As she says, she speaks English with an accent, and as she talks she looks at you, looking up from a filing cabinet, looking sideways as you walk with her. In addition to coordinating the Adult Secondary Education program, and influencing so much else in the adult school, Maria teaches mathematics, primarily to those preparing for the GED exam or a high school diploma. I understood the "no one can hide" comment during my first visit to Maria's class. She calls on students, particularly in the last rows where the reluctant sit. She jokes and pleads and hectors them to study, to do problems at home, to come see her. She goes person to person to lock in a meeting: "What time are you leaving today?" "Do you work every afternoon?" "Do you have Internet at home?" "Do you live around here?" Then: "OK, I want you to come see me at three o'clock." She and the counselor, Betty, will call people if they begin to miss school. "You all can do it," she says to the class, leaning forward, both hands on the desk. "Even if it is a nightmare, you can do it. But you have to ask for help." There is no escaping Maria.

In fact, Maria's identity in the classroom is one of the more complex blends of characteristics I've seen. She is a strong, methodical teacher. She is a coach and a cheerleader. She abides no nonsense, taking a young woman's cell phone ("unless you're an OB-GYN you don't need this now"). She is the moralizing aunt: "You're doing the same thing you did in high school. That's what got you here." She is a passionate advocate. She cares deeply. She laughs at herself and jokes with the class, and they joke back. And she works and works. A student sitting by me is close to tears, frustrated as she tries to do a problem that eludes her. Maria sees her, comes over, sets up a time to see her during a holiday break.

Though some of her students did well in school in other countries—and therefore have a solid basic education and a certain assurance about school—many went to school in the United States and, for various reasons, did not do well. School for them is not a pleasant place, and their fear, which can manifest as withdrawal or rejection, is quivering right beneath the surface. Nowhere is that fear more palpable than with mathematics. Given the history of failure and the anxiety that some of these students carry, it's quite a testament to willpower that they show up. Maria passionately wants to get through those emotional barriers: "It's a light crust," she says, "and once you crack it, you can make a change." I wonder whether that multifaceted persona of hers is the accumulation of all the different ways she's found to crack that crust.

The GED and high school diploma programs are test driven, and students prepare for the tests through math and English classes and through different levels of individual study in the Independent Learning Center, a large room filled with computers, books, filing cabinets, long tables, and chairs. This is also the place where students take most of their tests—units on science, units on math, all sorts of computer-based tests on language arts. So there is a good deal of back and forth between students at desks or terminals and teachers or aides going to filing cabinets or computer screens to check scores, monitor progress, offer direction. On some afternoons when students from different classes converge, the place is packed.

Given the importance of testing, it's no surprise that Maria focuses on test-taking strategies. "Read the question," she repeats. "Watch for what is being asked. Don't do everything right but forget to really look at the question." She gives her students problem after problem, making them read the problems out loud and state precisely what the problem requires. "They'll list answers that make sense if you misread the problem. So, think first!" She gives them tips based on experience: "The GED loves graphs or tables," or "You can bet there will be a question on scalene triangles." And she gives them problem-solving routines and shortcuts. Tricks of the trade. Sandra, the woman who teaches the class these students take in English, does a lot of the same kind of thing. They are trying to provide in a few months the academic know-how that students successful in American schools gain over years.

For some time now, Maria has been very much involved in a statewide project that provides instructional technology assistance for adult education. She has mentored other teachers, has taught online classes, has piloted new courses, and is helping to revise the program's website to make it more user friendly to other adult ed teachers. She says that doing this kind of work and coordinating the secondary education program "keeps my brain happy." And it's important to her that she does all this while staying in the classroom. "I'm not just sitting in some building far away creating curriculum." There is a grounded restlessness to Maria; she keeps pushing and pushing not only her students but herself and her program. How can it be made better? Some educators and policy makers are asking the same question of the GED exam on a broader scale.

Adult education normally gets little notice in policy-making circles or in the media—it lacks status or a powerful constituency—but it is the focus of attention now, particularly the GED. Every ten or fifteen years the developer of the GED exam, the American Council on Education—an advocacy and research organization that created the test during World War II for military personnel who didn't complete high school—revises the test, and as of early 2012 a major revision is in progress. A big concern is to bring the test in line with what students will need to know to attend college and thus reduce the number of remedial courses many students with GED certificates need to take, courses that jeopardize their chances of graduating. (By one estimate, only 10 percent of GED recipients earn a college degree.) This goal of increasing graduation rates is in line with a broader push in our nation to facilitate movement up the educational credentialing ladder—evident in community college circles where there is renewed emphasis on preparing students to transfer to four-year schools. The United States is a credentialing society. One hundred years ago, a high school degree was an unusual achievement (about 7 percent of the population held a degree), while today the postbaccalaureate credential or degree is expected if not required in many fields. The revision of the GED exam fits this pattern.

Approximately 40 million American adults don't have a high school degree or GED certificate, and if we want to meet the goals championed by policy makers to equip more of our citizens with some kind of postsecondary education, then we will have to tap that 40 million. Yet the revision of the GED exam, important as it is, does raise some concerns.

Education is delivered in a complex social system; changes in one domain will have an effect on what happens in others. Rethinking the GED exam as a measure of college readiness will make it harder to pass, which is not on its own merits a bad thing; raising educational expectations and preparing people for advancement will have some beneficial consequences. A previous revision added a writing sample to the multiple-choice questions, which overall led teachers to pay more attention to writing. But if standards are raised, what will happen to those low-skilled adults who struggle to pass the current exam—people, who, several studies suggest, stand to gain the most labor market benefit from a GED certificate? The test developers say that they plan to have two levels of passing the test, the traditional high school equivalency level and a new level indicating "college and career readiness." Fair enough, but the traditional level will thus be symbolically rendered even more of a second-class certificate.

The goal of the reformers is, in the words of one college president, to make the GED "an aspirational degree." But for some—like the woman I mentioned earlier who could come to school only one hour per day—the GED certificate already represents a monumental goal, aspiration more dogged and hopeful than many of us can imagine. Some low-skilled adults at this time in their lives do not have the finances, family arrangements, support systems, or work schedules that make any goal beyond passing the exam feasible. If we want them to achieve more, then we need to go way beyond the amping up of a test to provide more employment opportunities, child care and health care, and other social services—all of which are being cut back rather than enhanced. As we toughen up the GED exam, what will we make available to those for whom the old exam was barely within reach?

A number of the adult educators I spoke with expressed a further concern that the increased focus on the enhanced GED, especially in a time of limited—and shrinking—resources, will draw attention and funding away from the other sectors of adult ed. When we make programs more demanding, we also have to ensure that we have other programs in place to address the needs of those who risk getting left behind. Otherwise, we will continue to help the (relatively) better off at the expense of the truly vulnerable, keeping in place a sizable educational underclass.

At first glance, it seems that there are plenty of opportunities for undereducated adults to receive services—at least those living in medium- to large-size cities. Community colleges provide a range of basic-skills courses, and some students get their GED certificate while attending these institutions. There are the adult schools we've been considering. Some libraries offer literacy instruction and tutoring. There are churches and community-based organizations that offer basic education as well. It seems like we have a fair amount of duplication here with room for cutting costs.

To be sure, coordination among these institutions and agencies would be a good thing not only for economic efficiency but also to make life easier for recipients, for they often have multiple needs that could benefit from a consolidation of services. But these places are rooted in a particular social and organizational history and therefore each might draw on different populations of recipients and of paid and unpaid staff, so consolidation, though perhaps desirable, is politically and organizationally difficult to achieve. Furthermore, the scarcity of resources typically contributes to a competitive more than a collaborative ethos among these players. Also, and this is no small thing, each of these settings can have its own appeal to the adult who, it should be remembered, might feel a good deal of shame and reluctance about revealing low skills and seeking help. For those with painful memories of school, a church or local civic organization might be a safe space to start over.

Finally, and most striking, even with all these venues, only a small percentage of people in need are being served. A survey of one-third of the adult education programs in the United States reported 160,000 people on waiting lists for services in 2009–2010. A literacy program coordinator in New York City told me that of the 1.6 million adults in the city without a high school degree or GED certificate, only 60,000 to 80,000 are being served by all institutions combined. In some rural areas that I'm familiar with, the situation is even worse: there are few, if any, services available.

A major concern among economists and policy makers is whether the GED and other adult ed programs are worth the money. What is their "return on investment"? This concern is a primary driver of the current revision of the GED exam. GED recipients, as I just noted, often have to take a number of remedial classes when they enter college, their rate of degree completion is low, and some studies suggest that their success at finding a job is poor. University of Chicago economist James Heckman argues that the GED confers no labor market advantage. But other studies, drawn from Arizona to Michigan to Rhode Island and summarized in a new report from the McGraw-Hill Research Foundation suggest that adult education does provide economic benefit to the individual and to the local economy. These and further studies also point toward noneconomic social benefits: from improved health and health literacy, to reduced crime rates, to enhanced quality of life for the students and their families.

Because these social benefits tend to be given short shrift in our economically driven policy discussions, I'd like to dwell on them a bit. They *do*, in fact, have big economic consequences and, as well, take us to important questions about the good life and the good society. The social benefits of adult education and other compensatory and second-chance programs are particularly salient with people who have been living on the fringe of society, caught up in street life, violent or addicted or both, and, not infrequently, coming out of prison. When these people re-enter school, they are often walking right on the line, jumpy or sullen, wanting to make this work but at times terribly unsure that it will. And as the months progress and they slowly build occupational skill or gain proficiency in English and math or get interested in psychology or political science or literature—as they begin to *experience* this kind of achievement—then you start to see the transformation. Their demeanor changes. They develop confidence based on skill and knowledge ("I've never been able to build things," a construction trades student marveled). They calm down. They begin to draw a bead on the future. The crazy life on the streets can still call to them, and some give in, but others reject it and distance themselves from those who still live it. Along with that distancing come attempts to heal the awful wounds inflicted on families and to reunite with estranged children.

Still, adult education and literacy programs are threatened. "We're an endangered species," one director of an East Coast literacy program told me. That report from McGraw-Hill notes that the cost per student of adult education is about one-fourth to one-fifth of the cost of educating a student in the K–12 system. Still, the doubts among some legislators about the economic returns on adult ed are strong and threaten funding, especially in economic hard times dominated by demands for austerity. As I mentioned in the introduction, a draft of the upcoming year's budget for the Los Angeles Unified School District lines out the entire funding for adult education.

Hand in glove with the austerity perspective is a belief, held by many in positions of power, that those in adult education who went through American schools blew it the first time through, and so society should not have to pay again for what should have been learned already. (The same argument plays into funding for college remedial programs.) This belief clashes with the notion of the United States as a second-chance society.

This mix of fiscal skepticism and stigma affects the attention paid to and funding for the education and professional development of those who teach in adult schools and literacy programs. The teachers and tutors, a fair number of whom are volunteers, range widely in background, some with graduate degrees in the fields they teach, others with no formal education or training at all in teaching reading, mathematics, or science. The majority of teachers are part-time and have to have other jobs to make ends meet. Turnover rates are high. The default curriculum, then, becomes the traditional one, based on workbooks written for children. This lack of training is especially a problem for those who work with marginally literate populations, many of whom could have some sort of disability. I think back to that fellow in the Adult Basic Education class we observed earlier, the middle-aged African American man who is so motivated but, it turns out, is stuck on double consonants. Is he limited by some sort of linguistic processing difficulty, and, if so, what kind of training does his tutor have to help him address and compensate for it?

The creators of the new GED exam include professional development in their reform initiative, particularly the offering of online modules to explain the new format and content, but I wonder whether these modules will be more than an owner's manual. Will there be opportunity for teachers to discuss online what they do and where they're running into trouble, to interact with each other, to learn things beyond the new test format? Furthermore, will the new exam absorb whatever funds that are made available for professional development, leaving once again to their own devices the least educated and those who work with them?

———————

A few weeks before the Christmas holiday break at the adult school, Maria asks the students to post anonymously on the large, colorful bulletin board in the main hallway their thoughts as the year comes to an end and a new year looms. Over the week, more and more notes—some handwritten, some typed—appear across the red and green board:

> I hope that in the next year I improve
> even more than I did in 2011.

> I am really struggling to get my high school
> diploma, but I know someday I will.

> I am going to get more involved at my children's
> school to learn about their progress in
> their education.

> I am thankful for having such a blessed
> life. Without school I have no idea where
> I would be.

By the last day, the board is full.

As I've been visiting the adult school, I've been reading the criticisms of adult education along with articles on the revision of the GED exam. So much of the criticism has to do with quantifiable outcomes—pass rates, rates of enrollment in some postsecondary school or program, employment rates—and the targets of the criticism are the adult education and literacy programs themselves. This is legitimate criticism. The quality of instruction and tutoring across this complex landscape of services is highly uneven, and many of the people—for the most part, decent, committed people—who do the work have minimal training. And the curriculum used in many programs is outdated and limited. As I argue throughout this book, we as a society have to continue to work through our biases, our faulty notions about learning, our lowered expectations and do better by the educationally underprepared.

But we can't achieve this goal to any degree while funding to these programs is being cut. And we can't achieve the goal through educational programs alone. The people who enter adult education and literacy programs are typically facing a number of hardships: inadequate housing, sporadic or no employment, family disruption, problems with immigration, the criminal justice system. The best programs, so-called wraparound programs, provide multiple social and health services along with education, but most programs do not. Historian Harvey Graff coined the term *literacy myth* to characterize the belief that achieving a certain level of literacy alone will enable a person to overcome the hardships of poverty and discrimination. These days a lot of education reform at all levels seems to operate on this assumption and, for that matter, so do some literacy programs. To stay in educational programs and to thrive, people who carry a big burden often need help from agencies beyond the classroom.

I also worry that we will not develop powerful programs for those seeking a second chance with the kind of analysis that currently dominates education policy and the technocratic solutions that emerge from that analysis. As I noted, most of the policy studies of adult education seek to demonstrate economic effects of programs through statistical outcomes that can be readily defined and measured, such as the number of certificates or diplomas earned by those who passed the GED exam. Such information gives a broad view of trends, and I am not at all dismissing the importance of this perspective; however, such studies, because they deal in averages, often do not tease out important differences in programs or in participants, which get washed out in the aggregate. Take the GED examination as an illustration. A fair percentage of people prepare for the test on their own, so the amount of effort put into preparation and what they learn could vary widely. Those who enroll in a program might have quite a different educational experience regarding the GED, and recall that the quality and duration of programs vary widely as well. To make claims about the overall effectiveness of the GED examination without accounting for such variation is to miss the details that can mean failure or success.

There is another issue, and that is the fact that any statistical analysis taken alone is limited and, as good statisticians will tell you, can miss a lot. If a student quits a program before completing a certificate or degree, he or she is tallied up as a negative for the program. Yet what I've seen with some frequency is that people will leave once they develop sufficient skill to get a job. This has a positive economic impact, but in many analyses would register as a program failure. One more thing: This behavior—going for the short-term payoff—is often cited as an illustration of poor people's inability to delay gratification and form long-term goals. That's possible—people in all income brackets have problems with long-term goals—but in my experience, most of the people taking those immediate jobs do so because the rent is due, children need to be fed, members of the family are sick. They are quite aware of the trade-off and say they want to return to finish the program, for they could improve their long-term job prospects with more education. We'll see whether circumstances will permit a return, but it is absolutely not true that they left just to buy a few bright, shiny objects or to kick it with friends. We have such demeaning ways of talking about the choices poor people have to make when the wolf is at their door.

If our economic analysis can miss the mark, our understanding of the personal and social benefits of adult education programs is even more narrow. Few studies take us in close to people's lives. There's no reflection of the lady coming to class to keep her mind alert, of the man's posture changing over time as he begins to decode print, of the desire in those notes on the bulletin board. To be sure, these moments do not tell the whole story of the adult school, but they certainly tell us something beyond a general outcome measure. What we lack in the reports is the blending of the statistical table with the portrait of a life. Without both, we'll get one-dimensional policy fixes driven by numerical data removed from the daily lives of the people from whom the data are abstracted.

―――――――

Along the top of the north wall of the Independent Learning Center, right over a row of computer terminals, Maria has written out in big script her five goals for the program: Each student will be a lifelong learner . . . and a critical thinker . . . ending with a new goal that she is trying to enact through public events—a clothes drive, visiting senior centers—put on by the adult school:

> Each student will be able to participate and
> contribute as a citizen of his/her community.

Her work, finally, as she said to me one day, "is to help people grow and become full citizens in the world."

Maria's desk is in the front center of the room; the goals are up on the wall to her right. She is sitting alongside a young man who started but gave up on the essay portion of the GED exam. He is slumped down in the chair, but looking up at Maria, a knit cap, a pierced eyebrow, a gentle non-expressive face. "I think you gave up too early on your essay," she says, cocking her head slightly to the left to hold his gaze. "You got a high score on grammar. You can do this." She puts her hand on his shoulder, "No writing like text messaging. You're going to show the person who reads this all your knowledge." The fellow pushes his hands into his jacket pockets. "Come on, can't you squeeze one little essay out of you?" He takes this in for a moment, then his face warms into a slight smile. "Cool."

It happens one person at a time.

TWO

Who Should Go to College?

Unpacking the College-for-All Versus Occupational Training Debate

WHEN I WAS IN high school in the early 1960s, the curriculum was split into three tracks: an academic or college preparatory track, a general education track, and a vocational track. Upon entrance, students were placed in one of these on the basis of their previous academic records or a measure of ability, typically an IQ score. The curriculum directed the students toward a four-year college or university, possibly a community college; toward service or low-level managerial careers; or into blue-collar work. The curriculum also contributed powerfully to the school's social order. The college-bound were in student government, edited the newspaper and the annual, and at year's end had a thick list of activities under their class photographs. I swear, looking back on it all, that the college prep crowd walked around campus with an air of promise.

Since the mid-twentieth century, sociological and educational studies have documented the bias at work in the way students got placed in these tracks; for example, working-class and racial and ethnic minority students with records of achievement comparable to their advantaged peers were more frequently placed in the general ed or vocational tracks. And there was the more general concern that this way of educationally stratifying young people was simply undemocratic. The eminent American philosopher John Dewey called it "social predestination."

A remarkable amount of effort by educators, policy makers, advocacy groups, and parents has resulted over the last few decades in a dismantling of formal tracking. Although patterns of inequality still exist in the courses students take—vocational courses are overpopulated by poorer kids—we have in our time witnessed the emergence of a belief that college is a possibility for everyone. Today, however, we are also witnessing the rise of a strong counter-voice, skeptical about the individual and societal value of channeling all young people into postsecondary education.

The skeptics are a diverse group. Many are economists who point to trends in the labor market that reveal a number of good and growing jobs that require some postsecondary occupational training but not a four-year or even a two-year degree. Some are educators (including, but not limited to, Career and Technical Education interest groups) who emphasize the variability of students' interests and aptitudes, not all of which find fulfillment in a college curriculum. And some are social commentators who blend the economic and educational argument with reflection on the value of direct contact with the physical world, something increasingly remote in our information age. Though these skeptics come from a wide range of ideological backgrounds, they share a concern that in urging postsecondary education for everyone, we perpetuate a myth that personal fulfillment and economic security can be had only by pursuing a college degree.

This debate is an important one and is of interest to me because of my own history, but more so because it directly affects the kinds of students I've been concerned with my entire professional life: those who come from less-than-privileged backgrounds and aren't on the fast track to college. It also catches my attention because a book of mine, *The Mind at Work*, is sometimes used in the argument against college-for-all.

The Mind at Work is the result of a study of the cognitive demands of physical work, from waitressing and styling hair to carpentry and welding. Our society makes sharp and weighty distinctions—distinctions embodied in curricular tracking—between white-collar and blue-collar occupations, between brain work and hand work. But what I demonstrate is the degree to which physical work involves the development of a knowledge base, the application of concept and abstraction, problem solving and troubleshooting, aesthetic consideration and reflection. Hand and brain are cognitively connected.

From these findings I raise questions about our standard definitions of intelligence, the social class biases in those definitions, and their negative effects on education, the organization of work, and our nation's political and social dynamics.

Those who use *The Mind at Work* to champion some type of occupational education over a bachelor's degree zero in on a core claim of the book: that physical work is cognitively rich, and it is class bias that blinds us from honoring that richness. But I go to some length to tease out the historical and social factors surrounding this core premise, particularly as it plays out in the division between the vocational and the academic courses of study. I want to raise these issues again here, for they can get simplified in the debate between advocates of college-for-all and the skeptics. In fact, I worry that, as is the case with so many education debates, it will devolve into a binary polemic. The predictable result will be a stalemate or a partial and inadequate solution that will neither address the web of concerns that underlies this debate nor honor the lives of the young people at the heart of it.

Let me begin by acknowledging current labor-market realities, for many low-income students are in immediate financial need. These students can commit to any form of postsecondary education only if it leads to a decent wage and benefits. Furthermore, the record of postsecondary success is not a good one. Many students leave college without a certificate or degree that can help them in the job market, and, in many cases, they incur significant debt. There are good jobs out there that require training but not a two- or four-year degree, jobs that are relatively secure in a fluid global economy. The plumber's and the chef's work cannot be outsourced.

It is also true—and anyone who teaches, and for that matter, any parent, knows this—that some young people are just not drawn to the kinds of activities that make up the typical academic course of study, no matter how well executed. In a community college fashion program I've been studying, I see students with average to poor high school records deeply involved in their work, learning techniques and design principles, solving problems, building a knowledge base. Yet they resist, often with strong emotion, anything smacking of the traditional classroom, including the very structure of the classroom itself. This resistance holds even when the subject (textiles, history of fashion) relates to their interests.

The college-for-all versus occupational training debate is typically focused on structural features of the K–12 curriculum and on economic outcomes with little attention paid to the intellectual and emotional lives of the young people involved: their interests, what has meaning for them, what they want to do with their lives. A student in a welding program gave succinct expression to all this: "I love welding. This is the first time school has meant anything to me."

The problem is that historically the vocational curriculum itself has not adequately honored the rich intellectual content of work. As the authors of an overview of high school voc ed from the National Center for Research in Vocational Education put it: vocational education "emphasized job-specific skills to the almost complete exclusion of theoretical content." And the general education courses—English, history, mathematics—that vocational students took were typically dumbed down and unimaginative. Reforms over the past few decades have gone some way toward changing this state of affairs, but the overall results have been uneven.

The huge question then is this: Is a particular vocationally oriented program built on the cognitive content of work, and does it provide a strong education in the literacy and mathematics, the history and economics, the science and ethics that can emerge from the world of work? Few of the economists I've read who advocate an expansion of Career and Technical Education address the *educational* (versus job training) aspects of their proposals.

I want to return to the skeptics' concern about the mixed record of student success in postsecondary education. Do we really want to urge more students into a system that on average gradu-ates about 50–60 percent of those who enter it? But the skeptics' solution seems to fault students more than the colleges they attend and affords no other option but to redirect students who aren't thriving into job-training programs.

We need to be careful about painting this broad group of stu-dents with a single brush. Some are strongly motivated but be-cause of poor education, family disruption, residential mobility, or a host of other reasons are not academically prepared. The ques-tion is what kind of course work and services does the college have to help them. (And it should be noted that many vocational pro-grams recommended by the skeptics would require the same level of academic remediation.) Some students are unsure about their future, are experimenting—and in my experience, it's not easy to determine in advance who will find their way. We also know that a significant number of students leave college temporarily or per-manently for nonacademic reasons: finances, child care, job loss. Some of these cases could be addressed with financial aid or other resources and social services. So while I take the skeptics' point about the poor record of student success and agree that college is not for everyone and that a fulfilling life can be had without it, it is a simplistic solution to funnel everyone who is not thriving into a vocational program.

Such a solution also smacks of injustice. Right at the point in our society when college is being encouraged for a wide sweep of the population, we have the emergence of a restrictive counterforce that is seen by some as an attempt to protect privilege, or at the least, as an ignorance of social history. Research by sociologists

Jennie Brand and Yu Xie demonstrates that those least likely to attend college because of social-class position—and thus, on average, have a less privileged education—are the ones who gain the most economically from a college degree. For such populations, going to college can also provide a measure of social and cultural capital. A long history of exclusion must be addressed before countering broad access to higher education.

All the above raises the basic question: What is the purpose of education? Both the college-for-all advocates and the skeptics justify their positions on economic grounds, but another element in the college-for-all argument is that in addition to enhancing economic mobility, going to college has important intellectual, cultural, and civic benefits. These different perspectives on the purpose of college play into—and are shaped by—a long-standing tension in American higher education: a conflict between the goal of cultivating intellectual growth and liberal culture versus the goal of preparing students for occupation and practical life. I treat this issue more fully in other chapters in this book, but let me say here that I think this tension—like the divide between the academic and vocational—restricts the conversation we should be having. How can we enhance the liberal studies possibilities in a vocational curriculum and enliven and broaden the academic course of study through engagement with the world beyond the classroom?

A third option besides college or work has emerged in the last few years: Linked Learning, which is also known by its former name, Multiple Pathways. There are various incarnations of Linked Learning, but a common one is a relatively small school that is theme-based and offers a strong academic curriculum for all students; the students then have options to branch off toward a career, an occupational certificate, or a two- or four-year degree.

It is important to remember here that goals, expectations, and what students imagine for themselves are deeply affected by information and experience. For a pathways approach to be effective, students will need a lot of information about college and careers as well as multiple opportunities to visit colleges and potential work sites: hospitals, courts, and laboratories. The differences in cultural and social capital between students at prestigious research universities and the students I know at inner-city community colleges are profound and widening as inequality expands in our country. Pathways advocates will have to confront this inequality head on, for it is as significant as the construction of curriculum.

The college-for-all proponents would applaud the emphasis on a strong academic core but worry that this system could devolve into a new form of tracking. And the college-for-all skeptics, I suspect, would applaud the presence of a vocational pathway, though worry that antivocational biases would still stigmatize the option. These are legitimate concerns, and many advocates of the Linked Learning approach acknowledge them. These advocates also admit the significant challenges facing such a reform: from faculty development and curriculum design to the ancillary academic and social services needed to provide a quality prepathways education for all students. Still, this is a promising alternative, and some schools are demonstrating success with it.

Though this college-versus-work debate can slip into a reductive either/or polemic, I think that it does raise to awareness a number of important issues, central not only to education but also to the economy, to the meaning of work, and to democratic life: the skyrocketing cost of college and the poor record of retention and graduation in higher education, the disconnect between the current labor market and the politically popular rhetoric of "educating our way into the new economy," and the significant commitment of financial and human resources that will be needed to make college-for-all a reality.

On a broader scale the debate raises the issues of the purpose of education in a free society, the issue of the variability of human interests and talents, and the class-based bias toward entire categories of knowledge and activity—a bias institutionalized in the structure of the American high school. We need to rethink the academic-vocational divide itself and its postsecondary cousin, the liberal ideal versus the vocational mission of the college. And finally we need to keep in mind that the college-for-all versus occupation debate takes place within a history of inequality, and that the resolution of the debate will involve not only educational and economic issues but civic and moral ones as well.

THREE

Full Cognitive Throttle:
When Education for Work Ignites the Mind

As I EXIT THE freeway into the center of the overcast city, it is close to seven in the morning. A homeless man with a handwritten sign—"Vietnam vet"—stands at the bottom of the off-ramp. Behind him is a three-story building, the top floor burned out; big, fat-lettered graffiti covers the blackened name of the company. I turn left toward the parking lot of my destination, a community college serving one of the poorest parts of the city. I pass a small used-car lot, another boarded-up building, and several machine shops still in operation. The streets are gray and nearly empty. Then, on the right, the college and heightened activity. Cars and buses are pulling over to the curb to drop people off; students wearing backpacks weave their bicycles in and out of traffic; the light turns green, and a crowd that just got off a commuter train streams onto the campus.

After years of neglect, students like these—and the colleges that serve them—are the focus of national attention. Although many states are slashing education budgets, federal and private philanthropic initiatives are providing some help for people who are economically, and often educationally, disadvantaged to pursue further schooling. I play a tiny role in this effort as part of a research team that is trying to get a better handle on what enables or impedes educational success for this group. What makes it possible for these students to walk onto this campus an hour after sunrise, heading toward a nursing or electrical construction or English class? What jobs—if they have them—are flexible enough to allow time for school? Are these people going from here to work or coming in after the night shift? What child-care arrangements do they have? How about transportation? Although many of the college's students are local, a number come from fairly far away by bus or train to attend its well-respected occupational programs. One young woman I interviewed gets up at 3:30 in the morning to begin the trek to her 7:00 A.M. class. Hardships of that order are obviously threats to achievement. But I'm just as interested—more so, really—in what pulls these students forward, the desire that gets them through the door. I understand it just a little better every time I visit a place like this.

––––––––––

Come along with me for the first day of one of the college's programs for people who have low academic skills (many of them didn't finish high school) but who want to prepare for a skilled trade. The director of the program is standing at a lectern at the front of a large classroom; before her are twenty-five or so students sitting quietly in plastic chairs at eight long tables. The director has a serious demeanor, but her voice is inviting. Behind her hang an expansive whiteboard and a screen for PowerPoint or video presentations. I lean back and look around the windowless room: the walls are bare, institutional cream, clean and spare. The students are Black and Latino, a few more women than men. Most appear to be in their early twenties to early thirties, with one man, who looks like he's had a hard time of it, in his mid-forties. "Welcome to college," the director says. "I congratulate you." She then asks each of them to talk a little about what motivates them and why they're here.

The economic motive looms large. One guy laughs, "I don't want to work a crappy job all my life." A woman in the back says she wants to get her high school diploma "to get some money to take care of myself." But people give a lot of other reasons for being here, too: to "learn more," to be a "role model for my kids," to get "a career to support my daughter," to "have a better life." The director turns to the older man. "I'm illiterate," he says in a halting voice, "and I want to learn to read and write."

The semester before, when students wrote out their reasons for attending the program, the range of responses was even wider. Again, the economic motive was central, but there were also these comments, some written in neat cursive, some in scratchy, uneven print: "learning new things I never thought about before"; "I want my kids too know that I can write and read"; "Hope Fully with this program I could turn my life around"; "to develope better social skills and better speech"; "I want to be somebody in this world"; "I like to do test and essay like it is part of my life."

Combined, these testimonies offer a rich vision of the goals of education. Yet nearly every speech, policy document, and op-ed piece on educational initiatives aimed at poor people is focused wholly on schooling's economic benefits. Speaking in September

2009 at a community college in Troy, New York, President Obama said, "The power of these institutions [is] to prepare students for 21st-century jobs." Given the complex nature of the economy in our time—not only the recession but the changing nature and distribution of work—the people in this program certainly want the president's statement to be true. But they are also here for so much more. They want to do something good for themselves and their families. They want to be better able to help their kids with school. They want to have another go at education and change what it means to them. They want to learn new things and to gain a sense—and the certification—of competence. They want to redefine who they are. A lot is riding on this attempt to reenter school; no wonder, as I sit in this classroom, the hope and desire are almost palpable.

At the table right in front of me, a slight young woman with *Love* woven on the back of her black sweatshirt is leaning in toward the director as she talks. Whenever the director gives out a piece of information—about textbooks, about the tutoring center— the woman takes notes. I know from talking to many other students over the years the sense of excitement they feel at a time like this: a sense of life opening up but also the foreignness of it all, the uncertainty.

The director announces that it's time for a quick tour of the campus, and off we go to the bookstore, the administration building, the office for students with disabilities. The students walk in groups of two or three, talking, looking at this new campus landscape. A few walk alone. The young woman in the black sweatshirt stays close to the director. Toward the end of the tour, we pause before the child-care center. The director asks, "Who has kids?" A number of people say they do, raising their hands. The young woman slips her pen into the pocket of her *Love* sweatshirt and brings her hand slowly to her shoulder.

What my research team is finding so far about the possible barriers to success for students like her supports the research that's already been done. Students tend to drop out of school for reasons other than academics. Poor basic skills, especially significant problems with reading, make college very difficult. And students do flunk out. But the main reasons people quit have to do with circumstances beyond the campus: child care, finances, housing, and family disruption ranging from injury or serious illness to divorce or immigration problems. As I was writing this, I got a phone call from a student I've come to know—a young man doing well in one of the occupational programs—asking me if I had any leads on where he might go for housing or shelter. He was suddenly homeless and on the verge of dropping out of college. He wasn't alone. Three of his classmates were living in shelters near the campus. A fourth had been sleeping for several weeks behind the dumpster by the library.

No wonder that, along with the hope and sense of possibility they express, these students also voice, sometimes within the same sentence, the worry that this rug too will be pulled out from under them. Most of these students do not have a history of success, especially in school, and they want this time to be different, but if one thing goes wrong—an accident, getting laid off—there's little reserve to draw on.

Many of the occupational programs at the college have been in operation since the mid-twentieth century, if not earlier. One such program, welding, which sits farther into the heart of the campus, has provided generations of students with a powerful trade, enabling them to make a decent living. It's one of the programs where I have been spending a lot of my time.

The welding workshop is a huge room, rows of benches down the middle and sheltered stalls along the walls. Welding equipment—gas tanks, the consoles for different electric welding processes, cutting machines, vises and grips—is spread throughout the room; rows of pipes and conduits and vents are crisscrossed along the walls and overhead. Walk in during class and you'll think you've entered Vulcan's temple. Thirty or more students are practicing their techniques. Sparks fly up from the workstations, and from inside the stalls fiercely bright light pulses and dies. You'll need a mask to get close to the students. Everything is loud: the discordant symphony of welding's pops and crackles; the continuous hammering as the novice welders knock slag off their welds or peen a weld to improve its ductility. Voices rise above the din: the instructor tells one guy, and three others watching, to "look at your angle, man, look at your angle" and "don't push the electrode, glide it." Even with the vents, the strong, acrid smell of electrical heat fills the air. This is where knowledge and skill are forged.

Over two years, students will develop physical adroitness with welding's tools and attune their senses to welding's demands. They will become proficient in the use of various welding processes, each having advantages for different metals, structures, and conditions. They will learn about metallurgy and electricity. They will learn the vocabulary of welding and its many symbols and will develop a level of literacy and numeracy that enables them to read the welding code, pass certification exams, and function on the job. They will learn problem solving, troubleshooting, decision making—thinking in a careful and systematic way about what they're doing and why.

Not all vocational programs provide such solid preparation for a career, and even this program has felt strongly the effects of the recession. Although there are some jobs out there—in fact, the foreman from a campus construction site came into the shop recently looking to hire someone on the spot—those students who are mobile might have to move to other states to find employment. As with so many kinds of work, everyone is waiting for the economy to turn around.

I know that employment is the obvious goal of occupational programs, but I've also been struck by the other things the good ones make possible, the things that commentators rarely talk about. These programs provide a meaningful context for learning and a home base, a small community with a common goal. For many participants, school has not offered this kind of significance, and the results can extend beyond economic benefits to the kind typically associated with a more liberal course of study—yielding an education that first group of students I mentioned said they entered the college's basic-skills program to achieve.

Elias, Cynthia, and Bobby are pursuing both a certificate in welding and an associate of science degree. I've observed them in class, read their writing, and had a number of conversations with them, some focused on their education, and some just casual chitchat walking from one part of the campus to another. Not everyone in the program is as engaged by school as these three, but what is happening to them happens frequently enough to catch your attention.

Elias is in his first semester. In his mid-twenties, medium height and build, clean cut, he readily talks trash with the other men but just as easily becomes well spoken and reflective. I first noticed him in the basic-math class the welding instructor conducts before taking his students into the shop. The students work on the mathematics of converting fractions and of calculating area but also on solving word problems that involve welding. Elias was an eager participant, watching intently as his instructor laid out a problem, volunteering answers—some right, some wrong—then taking the instructor's feedback and looking down at the page, calculating again.

Elias's mathematical knowledge upon entering the program was at about the level of adding and subtracting simple fractions. The stuff he's doing now feels new to him, since he "checked out" of high school early on and eventually dropped out. During his late teens and early twenties he "ran the streets and was into drugs." But, and here his eyes widen as if waking up, one day he had this realization that he was going nowhere and wanted to turn his life around. He works as an entry-level car mechanic but, since he's single with no kids, wants to adjust his schedule to accommodate more schooling. "This is too important to me," he says. "I wish I didn't screw up before."

When she ran for an office in student government, Cynthia, one of the few women in the program, printed a flyer showing her in full welding garb—leather apron, gloves, mask flipped up to reveal her round face, almond eyes, and trace of a smile. The flyer read: *Vote 4 updating curriculum and equipment and for improving campus communication.* Her welding classmates distributed the flyers for her. She'd never done anything like this before, she told me. She'd never run for office in high school and had avoided any kind of public speaking. But as she was beginning her second year, her welding instructor—for reasons not entirely clear—pushed and prodded her to go on this political journey. His instincts were true. During the campaign, I was observing a class in another department when Cynthia visited to give her two-minute stump speech. She said she was running to fight for more resources and to get a student voice into a current conflict between the academic and vocational departments. Standing still in front of the room, her hands folded in front of her, she lacked the polish of some of the other candidates, but she was articulate and quietly passionate, the fluency that comes from authentic belief. She wanted to make a difference.

Bobby is about five foot eight, barrel chested, buzz cut, looks to be in his mid-to-late forties. He's completed the welding certificate but is still in school pursuing his academic degree and assisting in the welding program. You'll meet more than a few people like Bobby on this campus, in trouble with the law since he was thirteen: pills, meth, multiple incarcerations. About seven years ago during one of his times in jail, it came to him: "What am I doing? What's my life going to be?" He found religion and began the journey to various halfway houses and occupational centers. Then he found the welding program. Bobby has a jittery energy about him—his arms flap out from the sides of his body when he walks—but when he shakes your hand, it's with a full grip, and he looks you straight in the eye and holds the gaze. I remember thinking of those corneal scans in futuristic movies; he's taking your full measure in a blink.

Bobby asked me to read one of his English compositions; it was on leadership, using his elected position in the campus chapter of the American Welding Society as the main example. He insisted I give him my opinion and any suggestions as to how to make it better. I've also talked to him about an art history course he's taking, a general education requirement. He likes it, finds it interesting. We talked about a field trip he had taken to a museum. He was amazed that he could identify different styles and periods of art. Bobby's got what jazz musicians call "big ears"; he's wide open, curious about everything. "Not a day goes by," he said to me when we were talking about the art course, "where you don't learn something—otherwise, something's wrong with you."

Regardless of whether Elias has ever seen the kinds of math problems he's now doing—and given his chaotic school record, it's hard to know whether he has—he is engaged with them as if for the first time. Mathematics now means something to him. It is not only central to what he wants to do for a living, it has also become part of his attempt to redefine who he is. Cynthia, by running for office, is hurling herself into a political and rhetorical world that is new to her, an act of courage and experimentation. She is finding her way into institutional life and the public sphere, and in so doing she is acquiring an on-the-ground civic education. Bobby is in full cognitive throttle. After so many years of kicking around, chasing dope, bouncing in and out of jail, he's found solidity at the college, a grounding that frees him up in a way that he never knew on the streets. Yes, he's eager to finish up here and transfer to a four-year school, but he's taking it all in along the way—leadership, essays, museums.

Fostering this kind of learning and growth is in a society's best interest. What is remarkable is how rarely we see it depicted in our media, how absent it is in both highbrow and popular culture. Even more remarkable is how rarely our thinking and talking about education makes room for this vocationally oriented explosion of mind. As I noted earlier, it certainly isn't reflected in current education policy and politics. My worry is that if we don't see this kind of development, and if it's not present in our political discourse, then we won't create the conditions to foster and advance it.

Why are the experiences of the participants in that basic-skills program at the college or those of Elias, Cynthia, and Bobby not present in the public sphere? One reason, as I've said, is an education policy that for several decades has been so directed toward the economic benefits of education. Of the other goals of education that have formed the American tradition from Thomas Jefferson to John Dewey—intellectual, civic, social, and moral development—only the civic gets an occasional nod these days. The economic rationale is a reasonable political pitch, commonsensical and pragmatic, but students' lives and aspirations get reduced in the process.

A further piece of the puzzle has to do with social class. Few policy makers have spent much time at colleges that serve a mostly working-class population. And the journalists who write the stories we do occasionally read about such students tend to focus on their hardships and determination (which are worthy of depiction) or on their failures—which, sadly, are also true. What we rarely get, and maybe some journalists do not see, are the many positive educational dimensions of these students' time in school.

Another element connected to social class and deeply rooted in American educational history is the sharp distinction made between academic and vocational study, a distinction institutionalized in the early-twentieth-century high school. The vocational curriculum prepared students for the world of work, usually blue-collar, service, or basic-technology work, while the academic curriculum emphasized the arts and sciences and the cultivation of mental life. From the beginning, Dewey predicted the problems that this divide would create, and over the past three decades, school reformers have been trying to undo them: the artificial compartmentalizing of knowledge, the suppressing of the rich cognitive content of work, and the limiting of intellectual development of students in a vocational course of study. But Dewey's wisdom and reformers' efforts notwithstanding, the designation "academic" still calls up intelligence, smarts, big ideas, while the tag "vocational" conjures quite the opposite.

Related to the academic/vocational divide is the power of the liberal ideal, the study of the liberal arts for their own sake, separate from any connection to the world of work, crafts and trades, and commerce. The ideal has been with us since Plato and Aristotle: it has found full expression in Cardinal Newman's Victorian-era *The Idea of a University*, and it figures in discussions of higher education today as colleges and universities have grown and transformed, adding many majors outside of the liberal arts. One current example of this discussion is found in the widely reviewed book by Andrew Hacker and Claudia Dreifus, *Higher Education? How Colleges Are Wasting Our Money and Failing Our Kids—and What We Can Do About It.* Hacker and Dreifus rightly criticize higher education for a host of sins: cost, production of endless esoteric research, exploitation of adjunct teachers. What is telling is that the model they offer to get college back on track is pretty much Cardinal Newman's.

Their assumption is that anything vocational cannot lead to, in their words, a liberation of imagination and the stretching of intellect. How interesting that in this bold evaluation of the state of higher education, their solution fits into the well-worn groove of the academic/vocational divide, denying the intellectual and imaginative possibilities of any course of study related to work.

Elias, Cynthia, and Bobby have the ability to pursue a liberal studies curriculum, and I suspect they'd find much there to engage them. But in their present circumstances, they couldn't follow such a course exclusively. It is precisely its grounding in work and its pathway to decent employment that makes their educational journey possible. Their vocational commitment doesn't negate the liberal impulse but gives rise to it.

When Cynthia was delivering her stump speech in that class I observed, she spoke about the political discord on campus between the academic and vocational faculty and pledged to try to do something about it. "I'm in welding," she said, "but I'm pursuing an associate's degree, too. These don't have to be in conflict. I want to unite that gap." Cynthia was talking about conflict over turf and resources, but that conflict arises from a troubling history of philosophical claims about knowledge and intellectual virtue. Speaking from her experience, she was onto something that eluded her elders. Her life and the lives of the other students we've met demonstrate that habits of mind, reflection and thoughtfulness, exploration and experimentation can be sparked both in classrooms and in the workshop, reading a book and learning a trade. We ourselves have to be more creative in fusing book and workshop for those who go to school to fashion a better life.

FOUR

Who We Are:

Portraits from an Urban Community College

I. Remedial English

"*Forlorn,*" the instructor, Mr. Quijada, asks, looking up from the essay the class is discussing. "What's *forlorn* mean?" "Desire," says the older man in the middle of the room—glasses, graying dreadlocks pulled back—then in the same breath adds "longing." "Close, Leonard," Mr. Quijada replies. "Longing can certainly lead to being forlorn." Casually strategic, Mr. Quijada looks to the last row. "Kimberly, it's good to see you back. Do you want to add to Leonard's definition?" Kimberly shakes her head, softly says "no," and looks to the young woman in the hoodie next to her who answers, "Sad; it means to be sad."

This is Basic English, the most basic of the three remedial English courses on campus. Upon entering the college, students take a standardized, multiple-choice placement test in grammar, reading comprehension, and mathematics. This test can clear them to take the credit-bearing, transferrable courses in English or mathematics or, as is the case for most of the students at this college, slot them into some level of remedial course work.

There is a lot of attention being given to remediation in college: think-tank policy papers, legislation in state houses, philanthropic initiatives, the media. There are reports on the high numbers of students who require remedial course work, on the threat remediation poses to postsecondary education, on the economic consequences both for taxpayers and for the nation's economic competitiveness. It is not good news, rendered primarily through institutional data—numbers of people held for remedial classes, pass and fail rates—with occasional brief profiles of students who are struggling. It is a huge problem that so many students are not prepared for college-level work, an indictment of our educational system, and a symptom of broader inequality as well. The reports and articles don't give us a very good sense of who these students are—and they are a widely varied lot—so let us learn more about them, beginning with Mr. Quijada's class.

The class currently includes thirty students, though originally there were close to forty. A lot of adding and dropping goes on in the first week, and when some students saw the amount of writing Mr. Quijada assigns, they looked for another section. The ages range from nineteen, right out of high school, to two people in their fifties. There are a number of reasons they are here. Some have had poor educations, and some are still learning to write English. Some have a learning disability, a difficulty processing written language. A student with a hearing impairment sits in front with a signer. Some have been away from school for a long time and haven't taken a standardized test in decades. And some— more than you might think—are misplaced. Some students write and read pretty well but test poorly. And some, unaware of the significance of the test, take it quickly and haphazardly, eager to get it over and get onto the next thing on their list: the counseling office, financial aid, child care, or work. Hardly anyone knew about the test beforehand, and no one prepared for it.

For their first assignment, Mr. Quijada asked his students to write a short essay about the main obstacle that might prevent them from passing the class, and, even with the reduction of spelling errors via spell-check, the papers reveal quite a range of skill. Two are deeply flawed: "When i am coming to school transportation sometimes may distract me because I don't pay attention to the time I have to get to class." At the other end of the spectrum are competent essays with stylish touches ("Sweet, blue, hard on the rocks liquor takes a hit on my five senses.") and well-crafted sentences and paragraphs. "Just the thought of going to class every day with a bunch of fresh faced students who just graduated from high school, and are probably the age of my granddaughter, had me sweating like I had just run a marathon." The rest fall somewhere in between: some with sentence fragments, some with problems in phrasing, some not well developed.

The features of their writing tell a story about the education these students had before coming here and the struggles many of them have had with writing. "The loss of education," wrote the woman who declined to answer Mr. Quijada's question, "is such a sad thing."

The content of the essays gives a glimpse into their lives right now. Five or six write pretty frankly about scaling back on club life or on sports, video games, and overall hanging out—consider that homage to blue liquor, hard-on-the-rocks. But all the rest, whether written as a formulaic school paper or written from the heart, reveal weightier challenges. Several express concern about their poor skills, how hard writing and reading and studying have been for them. One young woman writes about the loss of her family and subsequent struggles with depression—"How can I live without my parents?" Some write about trying to provide for their families, and two single parents wrestle with pursuing their own education without compromising the care of their children: "I want to succeed in life," but "I will sacrifice anything for my child."

The obstacles most students mention have to do with money: rent, bus fare, a car breaking down, gas for your brother who brings you to school. People with families worry about child care. Others mention school supplies, books, and for those who have computers, the price of ink for the printer. Internet fees and phone bills are an issue—I know from trying to reach students attending the college how often Internet or phone service is temporarily shut off. And a lost job or health crisis would be devastating. One or two bad breaks could destabilize their plans for school. There's little room for mishap.

Yet the desire in the essays, the can-do optimism is striking. You can attribute some of it to the school-paper formula: end on an up note. And there's a big dose of positive thinking here that can gloss over the depth and degree of challenge some of these students face. The record of success for those placing in the low-level skills courses is not at all good; according to one study, only 16 percent of students at this level complete the entire remedial sequence. Still, they write of "taking one step at a time," of "learning from my mistakes," of "not allowing friends and family to come between me and my dreams," of being "prepared" and "positive." "By taking this English class," writes a single mother who was laid off last year, "I will become a better writer and I will get the skills that I need to reach my goals in life."

If you leave this classroom and visit some of the other basic-skills courses nearby or the various tutoring and student assistance centers a few buildings away, you'll hear similar resolve. Fan out to the occupational programs along the perimeter of the campus—from fashion to diesel to nursing—and to the workforce development programs created in partnership with the city or with private industry. You'll hear resolve and hope there, too. And you'll hear the same litany of challenges—and a few more.

Some students are teetering between the streets and the classroom, and some have been through the criminal justice system. In one remedial math class that I observed, several students had to leave midway to recharge their ankle bracelets. Some students struggle with addiction, and some are in rehab. Some students live in violent and chaotic households, and some are homeless. As one instructor put it: "The fact that some of our students get here daily is a success."

And these students are the fortunate ones.

On the streets right outside the campus, you'll find people, many of them young, hanging out at midday, no work, no school. There are some small machine shops close by, but none are hiring. There's a fast food restaurant—not hiring. Within a few blocks you'll find a homeless shelter, single-room occupancy apartments, empty buildings that once held local industries. Drive a little farther and things get worse: dilapidated houses; empty lots with old cars, couches, mattresses; streets that are pitted and empty. There are similar layouts and demographic patterns in the core of most American cities. Things look different in rural America, of course, but the paucity of jobs and the patterns of unemployment are similar—often worse.

———————

What makes it so difficult to fulfill the desire that brings these people to college? Mr. Quijada's students gave us one cluster of potent reasons. Though students from advantaged backgrounds take remedial courses—in one study, 24 percent of students from the top socioeconomic quartile were enrolled in a remedial course— Mr. Quijada speculates that in his ten years at the college, he's taught maybe a dozen people from well-to-do families. The rest have been pretty much like the people in the class I observed. So whatever decisions Mr. Quijada's students make—wise or unwise, productive or counterproductive—they are made in the context of limited resources, sometimes profoundly limited resources. "A lot of my students," Mr. Quijada tells me, "are going through hell in their personal lives."

These are the current economic and social barriers to academic achievement, but other barriers began much earlier. There is a kind of knowledge and know-how about college that is acquired directly as a result of parents' social class, educational level, and social networks. I know this from my own experience.

Because of where and how I grew up, I had minimal exposure to middle-class homes, and it wasn't until well after college, once

I had been teaching, that my access to such households became more routine. On a visit to some college friends, I spent a little time with their two kids. Each boy had his own room, and each was seated before his computer. The rooms were appointed with bookshelves along one wall, and these were filled with fiction and nonfiction, some lightweight stuff, but good adolescent novels, too, and a number of reference books. Alongside each computer were a sophisticated calculator, a standard college *Webster's Dictionary*, and a thesaurus. (Today that computer would be supplied with a number of aids to literacy and numeracy and would have high-quality Internet access. The boys would have smart phones and possibly iPads.) The boys' parents were able to help them with just about any subject, any assignment, and the boys were able to learn a lot about using the computer for academic purposes by watching their parents, who used their own computers (the third and fourth in the house) for a variety of work-related tasks.

As I found out early the next morning, the parents had arranged their schedules such that each child could be driven to music or athletic practice before school and tutoring or some other academic program after. The boys had traveled overseas. And each was slated to spend a part of the summer in an enrichment program, one in the arts, one in science.

It was wonderful to see my friends, and the evening was full of laughs and reminiscence. But the boys' rooms affected me as soon as I crossed their thresholds, immediate, more visual and emotional than analytic. How completely, utterly different from my childhood home. To see advantage so clearly, so stark, and in this benign setting, well intentioned, decent, two sweet kids.

These two boys are learning a lot at home that is directly related to academic success, and their parents—and the people they hire—provide an entire program of (technologically rich) instruction that augments what the boys are learning at school. In addition to knowledge and skills, the boys acquire over time from their parents—who both have graduate degrees—and their parents' friends all sorts of information and understanding about college, about preparing for it, about its structure and conventions, about what it's like to be there. As college gets closer, they will be privy to specific information about application, scholarships, and course selection. Furthermore, whole counseling and tutoring industries have sprung up to ensure college readiness for the children of parents who can afford their services. They also gain the sense—and this is huge—that they belong in college, can thrive there, will enjoy and benefit from it. All this is in the air they breathe.

Not all middle-class and affluent parents devote this kind of time and resources to their children's education, and some do but in ways that create a whole host of problems. Also, I want to emphasize that many working-class parents place great weight on education and support their children's schooling in whatever ways they can. They engage in the same processes as do wealthier parents, for example, utilizing their social networks. In the interviews I've done at the college where Mr. Quijada teaches, a number of students spoke of parents going to some length to enlist family, co-workers, or church members to help them transfer their children to better schools or to get information about college admissions and scholarships.

The difference between parents like those college friends I visited and the parents of Mr. Quijada's students—or my parents—doesn't lie in basic goals or processes, but in financial resources, in experience in American higher education, and in the depth and breadth of information about college. My parents bought me what they could—a chemistry set, a telescope—and they told me from as early as I can remember that they wanted me to go to college. My mother also asked people at the restaurant where she worked about college. But my father had a year or two of elementary school, and my mother had to quit in the seventh grade. They couldn't help me with homework, or hire a tutor, or assess the quality of my education, or provide any specific information about college. And even with an extraordinary amount of help from my high school senior English teacher, I was still pretty much a duck out of water during my first year of college. These are the effects of social class.

Another huge factor in being prepared for college, of course, is the quality of your K–12 education. A lot of low-income students entering community college come from schools that are struggling. For a whole host of reasons—from inadequate resources, neighborhood economic decline, and limited health and social services to poor facilities, inexperienced teachers, and minimal (if any) honors and advanced-placement courses—students leave with subpar writing and mathematics skills and a thin or fragmented knowledge of core subjects: history, science, literature. And while some of what's involved in being prepared for college involves these traditional bodies of knowledge and skills, there are also other kinds of knowledge that are less clear-cut and obvious.

Around the same time I was observing Basic English, I was also spending time in the college's fashion program. I was talking with a young woman in a pattern-making class about a skirt she was designing. She was deeply committed to fashion, "loved" it, and had her own blog on an industry website. She told me with some excitement that a few days before she had gone back through her notebook to find some information she thought would help her with her current project. When I asked how she normally would have gotten such information, she said she would ask the instructor. But she had this flash of insight that her notebook was one of her resources, that the notes she routinely took as part of "doing school," and perhaps read over before a test, were actually *useful*.

When you start teaching at a college such as the one we're visiting—or, for that fact, at a lot of colleges—you soon notice some student behaviors that are puzzling, even strange, certainly counterproductive. There are students who have trouble keeping track of assignments and deadlines. Some misjudge—at times by a wide margin—the time it will take to do an assignment, or they work like crazy on one assignment and let others slide. Their notetaking is erratic or sparse or in some way not efficient or effective, yet some might think they're taking good notes. They don't ask questions, don't seek help, don't go to your office hours, even when you underscore the need to do so. There is a frustrating passivity to them. Part of what is puzzling is that some of the students in question—like the young woman in the fashion program—seem committed to their education. You can't chalk up their behaviors to a lack of motivation or engagement.

As with any complex practice—from baseball to weaving to singing opera—you learn how to do it well by doing it and doing it over time, typically in some sort of formal or informal setting with guidance and feedback from others who are more skilled. The same holds for learning how to be a student in the formal setting of school.

Over the years I've come to understand that a key dimension of underpreparation is that some students have learned how to attend school in a routine and superficial manner but haven't had the kind of education that teaches them not only bodies of knowledge and literacy and numeracy skills but also how to use their mind in certain systematic and strategic ways, how to monitor what they're learning and assess it, and just the tricks of the trade for functioning effectively in this place called school.

We typically talk about this sort of thing in terms of "study skills" and "time management," and we attempt to remedy problems related to such issues through orientation programs or workshops. And students can learn useful things in them. But the focus tends to be on techniques—how to schedule your day, how to highlight a textbook—while what I'm after here is something that includes techniques but is more of an orientation to learning, a way of being in school. So what can seem like a lack of engagement or lack of focus can more accurately be understood as some of the results of a less-than-optimal education.

In Mr. Quijada's Basic English class, it turns out that several students—including the older gentleman who volunteered to define *forlorn*—dropped the class because they couldn't master its auxiliary online platform. Two more students just stopped coming. Of the remaining twenty-five, eight didn't pass. They missed too many classes or didn't do the assignments or did poorly on them. Many who did pass followed Mr. Quijada into the next course in the remedial series, and some of them did well—including the young woman who wrote of her depression and the older woman who had been laid off. But one single mother quit to take a job; another young woman who was doing good work got pregnant and dropped the class right at the end of the semester.

As I noted, this level of attrition is common—especially for students who are required to take multiple remedial courses—and creates an awful situation for all concerned. For the institution, it is inefficient and expensive and signals a failure of its mission. For committed teachers like Mr. Quijada, it is sad and frustrating, and while in some cases it can lead to a productive reevaluation of one's teaching, it can also wear away one's sense of competence and the satisfaction one gets from the work. For the student, this kind of failure and dropping out results, at the least, in lost time and resources. Education is derailed. And along with the educational and economic liabilities, the hit on one's hopes and identity can be devastating.

Failure rates such as these lead to calls—from governors and legislators, academics and pundits—to reconsider and possibly narrow the wide mission of the community college, including its open admissions policy. And some observers question the nation's recent college-for-all ideology, as we saw in Chapter Two.

The critics of college-for-all are right in claiming that some students come to college without clear goals or direction—or for reasons that don't have much to do with a college's mission. Because of the open-door policy of most community colleges, there are students who arrive with such limited academic skills that, even with basic-skills courses and tutorial support, their chances of success are minimal. Other students enroll in college because they aren't sure what else to do. They couldn't find a job; their parents pushed them; their friends were going. With an uncertain future and few options, why not college? My own first thoughts about what I should do after high school fit this profile. Two of my buddies were going to go to a nearby community college to play football, and I figured I would go too—at least I'd know someone there. And some people enroll in college, particularly the community college, to get a financial aid award. They stay a few weeks and quit coming.

Yet other students might have a specific goal in mind, a major or an occupation, but have a thin or inaccurate understanding of the course of study or the demands of the trade. They don't have the experience or the social networks that would enhance that understanding. A student who wants to be a social worker signs up for sociology, not aware of what the academic study of sociology entails. Or the fashion program gets students who watch *Project Runway* and decide to be a fashion designer, not knowing about the countless hours of demanding, painstaking work it takes to develop competence.

These are examples of types of people who arguably shouldn't be going to college—at least at this stage of their lives. But they are also examples of the failure of other institutions in our society—or the lack of an appropriate institution at all—to help young people develop into adulthood. Students who come to college with fuzzy goals have probably had minimal counseling in high school. (Some beleaguered schools have a student-to-counselor ratio of 800 to 1, or worse.) As for those young people with an unrealistic or incorrect understanding of a course of study or occupation, if their high school can't provide such an orientation and if their family networks do not give them access to good information, where can they get it? Other than the high school, the only large-scale organizations focused on adolescents are the ones trying to sell them something.

As for those coming to college to collect financial aid, doesn't that practice to some degree reflect weakness in economic policy and inadequacies in the social safety net? Several quite successful students who came out of Mr. Quijada's classes revealed to me that they've had to use their financial aid money to pay medical bills or keep their parents afloat.

Acknowledging all the above, it is still a significant problem that a number of students attend for the wrong reasons, and I don't want to minimize the toll on resources and faculty. But it is important to point out that, in some cases, these students find their way. Once you're on the campus, picking up a sense of the place, meeting people, being exposed to new ideas, feeling the pull of opportunity, surprising things can happen. An instructor at another community college across town tells this story: An honored African American studies professor died, and the college put on a memorial for him. One of the speakers was a guy who explained that when he got out of prison and was kicking around, he decided he wanted to fix up his car. He found out that he could get financial aid, which he then used to buy a coveted set of chrome rims. During his first term, he enrolled in a course from the professor, and it drew him in. He took another, and the older man began to mentor him. He continued in school and got his associate's degree. Even a guy setting out to scam the system can get turned around.

I've taught for a very long time in a wide range of settings, kindergarten through graduate seminar, poor urban school to wealthy research university, and one thing I've learned is that there's usually more to a student's poor academic performance than meets the eye. The man who falls asleep in class is working a night shift to support his family. The young woman who doesn't turn in assignments worries to the point of physical distress about revealing her poor writing skills. The guy who seems distracted, unfocused, flaky even, is wrestling with parental expectations about his major. The class clown; the sullen, withdrawn type; the girl who's above it all, *whatever*—they all have something else going on.

We tend to characterize these behaviors in a shorthand way, a way that both describes them and implies causation. A student "lacks motivation," or isn't "serious," "committed," or "disciplined," or is "unfocused" and "scattered," or is "immature," maybe "lazy." We've done this sort of thing for a very long time. Early nineteenth-century educators referred to the poor common school performer as a "shirker" or "loafer"; in the last half of the nineteenth century the terms shifted a bit from a student's character to development and intelligence: the poor student was "immature," "sleepy-minded," "dull." As we move through the twentieth century we get a wide range of terms, from "dullards" to the more sociological "alienated" and "socially maladjusted." And so it goes. This kind of labeling is a very human thing to do; we all resort to it and in all kinds of contexts: within our families, at work, and in the public sphere. It's one of the many ways, for better or worse, we make quick sense of a blooming, buzzing universe. But I do believe that this way of describing academic performance can blinker our analytic vision. Such terms lead us to think we know more than we do about a student's behavior and circumstances and thereby limit our ability to create effective interventions. Finally, the terms are just not that helpful.

Remediation in higher education has been present in some form since the mid-nineteenth century; the fledgling University of California, for example, required that 50 percent of its students take a writing course to bring them up to par. Remediation is not new, and unless we have an unprecedented transformation of our social order and educational institutions, it will be with us for some time to come. As long as we continue to hold onto the ideal of educational opportunity, we will need remediation to help correct an imperfect educational system. It is true, though, that some community colleges have seen an increase in the number of students requiring remediation. There are many reasons for the increases—growing economic and educational inequality, the societal push for postsecondary education, more people seeking some small advantage in a rapidly changing economy—and those reasons lead a wide range of people into the community college remedial classroom. But in many reports, and particularly in popular portrayals, students needing remediation are represented as a great mass of the unprepared.

To respond fully and well to them, we have to know them better, move beyond the ready-made labels and explanations and understand how they got into classrooms like Mr. Quijada's, what exactly it is they need from us, and how to draw on their strengths and the many experiences and qualities they bring with them. One of the student leaders at the college put it so well: how can we come "to see students not necessarily as what they are not, but as what they could be?"

In that next course in the remedial series taught by Mr. Quijada, one of his students wrote for a first assignment about his return to college. He had been working regularly and had not been in school for many years, had no desire for it. Then the unexpected happened: He got laid off. Despondent, ashamed, his head bowed, he went to talk to his brother, who encouraged him to go back to school. Why not? It's now or never. He did and discovered he liked it. Three or four months later his brother called him, forlorn, to tell him that *he* had just been laid off too. Well, the student said, you should join me, come back to school. "So I'm glad he took my advice. If not, he would not be sitting next to me writing this paper."

Now, that's something to write about.

II. Occupational Education

The head of the hospital bed is elevated so that the mannequin is sitting upright, mouth open, an IV pole to the left, a table and tray to the right, a chair at the foot of the bed for visitors, a bulletin board in the mannequin's line of sight. *Hello!*, in bright letters extends across the top of the board, *the day is* _____. Cards from imaginary well-wishers are tacked below. This is the simulation room where student nurses administer medications to the patient, take vital signs, hook up an IV, and answer anxious questions posed by the instructor, Ms. Green, who sits behind a curtain watching the student on a video monitor.

Right now it's Molly's turn. Ms. Green is explaining that the patient, a Mrs. Bowman, is scheduled for a thyroidectomy. Molly, who is in the second semester of a four-semester program, listens, her hands across her belly. Then she nods, smiles, knocks on the wall, and walks out from behind the curtain into the hospital room. "Good morning, Mrs. Bowman, I'm Molly, your nurse for today. Nice to meet you. How are you feeling?"

"Well," the instructor says, channeling Mrs. Bowman, "I've never had surgery before, and I'm kinda worried."

"I understand. I do," Molly says, moving to the side of the bed. "Do you have any questions for me?"

Mrs. Bowman: "What should I expect after the surgery?"

Molly: "Well, you'll be fatigued, and it will be hard to swallow. So we'll keep you upright. We'll monitor you."

Mrs. Bowman: "What will the nurses be looking for?"

Molly: "We'll be looking for infection. We want to be sure you're draining nicely."

Mrs. Bowman says that her doctor told her some things, but she forgot, and begins to ask Molly about the features of the disease, and Molly knows a fair amount about it, but draws a blank on several symptoms. The patient, still concerned, returns to possible complications beyond infection, and Molly mentions swelling but admits she can't think of the others, but, er, will get back to Mrs. Bowman. Then it's time to debrief.

Molly walks back to the video monitor, shaking her fists in the air. "I studied everything but *that!*" Ms. Green tells her she did well—it is her first time, after all—that she has a nice way with patients, and that she needs to read up on the disease itself. They talk a little about monitoring the patient's calcium levels after thyroid surgery and then settle in to look at the video of Molly and Mrs. Bowman.

————————

Students do talk in the sewing room, small talk while cutting fabric or pinning the panels of a garment on a form, or just as often, they talk about their projects and lend each other a hand. And sometimes, like right now, all you hear is the sound of craftwork: the staccato bursts of sewing machines, the rustling of the paper on which students draw their patterns, the tearing of muslin, two or three people flipping through the pages of fashion magazines, and the intermittent *hiss* of the steam irons by the door. The large room looks industrial, long worktables and machines, fluorescent lights, old posters, and lots of magazine pictures of high fashion taped or pinned on faded cream walls. But as you walk slowly station by station in this class of advanced students, the concentration, the pushing of one's skills, is as vibrant as the purple and copper and brilliant green fabric splashing across the tables.

One student is meticulously stitching onto a piece of sheer fabric little silver tubes, following a sketch she's placed under the material. They will form a series of delicate fans. "I found some ready-made patterns like this in diamonds," she explains without taking her eyes off the work, "but I didn't want diamonds—and the color wasn't quite right. So I knew I had to do it myself."

Another student is pinning a piece of black gauze across the back of a form. It's gathered at the shoulder and fans out as it extends to the waist. This will cover another fabric on an "after five" dress, and he explains how he had to recalculate his original measurements so that he doesn't have "so much gather that you won't be able to see the fabric underneath."

At the next table, a student has before her a drawing of an evening gown, and she is erasing and sketching, erasing and sketching—rethinking the straps. Then she goes on to the bottom half of the gown, and she moves various paper cutouts across the table. She looks up and down from bust and straps to hem and finally sits back, tossing her pencil onto the table. Minutes pass. She raises her eyebrows, nods her head, picks up the pencil, and erases the straps.

Over by the door, a student is adjusting and pinning a black cocktail dress on a form. She explains that she had never worked with this fabric before and ended up having to change her design because the fabric was unforgiving. She pulls out her original drawing to show that though the base is the same, she had to redesign the top. It was over the weekend when she put the first version on a form she has at home and "ended up staring at the dress all day. The lines needed to make sense in the back, and they just didn't."

"So you're at the middle of the bus's chassis," Mr. Franco says, walking out from behind the podium, "and you're getting a weak reading on your meter. But, you know, the problem could be twenty feet away, up in the bulkhead. How would you find out?"

Mr. Franco is taking his students in the Diesel Technology Program through a long series of troubleshooting procedures. There are about thirty men packed into the square room, long tables in a U-shape along the perimeter, and three shorter tables inside the U. The men range in ages from early twenties to mid-forties; some are in the program after kicking around in short-term, dead-end jobs while others had decent work that went south when the economy tanked. Most have some interest in cars—usually from a young age—and some are mechanics, but most are new to diesel, drawn to it because of employment opportunities.

The classroom sits atop a giant automotive shop and is cold and spare, except for Mr. Franco's elaborate computer equipment, which he uses to animate diesel technology. The students all have laptops—their own or on loan from the program—that they use in concert with Mr. Franco's lectures and also to take exams from the lectures and from the textbook, the hefty fifth edition of *Heavy Duty Truck Systems*, full of dense print on chassis electrical circuits, hydraulics, driveshaft assemblies, transmissions, and a whole lot more. Some students have three or four highlighters of different colors on the table by their books. They also use the laptops for engine diagnostics once they tromp down a flight of bare metal stairs to the shop below where truck cabs, hoods open, and large engines up on stands await them. Long panels in the middle of the shop lay out and label the components involved in ignition, braking, air supply, and other key diesel systems. Mr. Franco illustrates his lectures here, and the students use the panels to test their developing knowledge, injecting air, for example, into sections of the brake board assembly to see which valves close. The big test, though, is troubleshooting problems with the various engines that Mr. Franco has disabled, writing up a diagnosis and list of parts needed for repair, then actually doing the repair to see whether the engine runs. As one of the students said to me, there's no bullshitting that test.

I spent close to two years visiting the occupational programs at this college, each one providing an entrée into a whole world of traditions, complex practices, and standards of excellence. Some people came into these worlds with knowledge of them already—they had worked in a doctor's office or were proficient with a sewing machine—and, in some cases, had a deep emotional connection to the occupation. One nursing student put in her binder a cutout of a nurse she had made in kindergarten. Some students enroll after high school, but most have had other jobs, were unemployed, or had been out of the labor market raising children. Some occupations draw heavily from community college programs such as these: 60 percent of new nurses, for example, come from them. In all cases, this new profession holds the promise of a better job and, with luck, a career with some stability.

The programs are demanding—the textbook for Medical-Surgical Nursing, a two-semester course, is 2,500 pages long—

and some have pretty high attrition rates. Fashion, a two-year program, loses about 50 percent of its students by the second year. Many students have families and other big-time responsibilities; there are always a few guys in the diesel program nodding off because they are coming to class right after working the graveyard shift. Without financial aid or unemployment insurance or a few small scholarships, a lot of students would not be able to attend at all.

Those who succeed develop powerful skills and bodies of knowledge: facts about physiology or diesel combustion and a range of techniques and tricks of the trade—but also ways of thinking and habits of mind, at least within the occupation.

I am struck, for example, by the careful attention paid to mastering very small but fundamental skills and developing a watchful, methodical approach to them. One of the student nurses close to getting her RN put it well: "It's the simple stuff that makes the difference." Hooking up an IV bag is a good example because of the many simple (but cumulative) steps: how to hold the bag, how to hold the insert tube, sterilizing the ports, getting air out of the tubes, clamping, labeling the tubes, double checking the contents of the bags, and so on. When the students first try it, they are maladroit or forget steps, and they practice and practice, "trying to put it all together in my head," as one expressed it. Then it does come together. They can do it over a sink, then on a mannequin, then eventually under supervision on the hospital floor. They understand the principles behind it. And they will get to the place where they incorporate this skill into broader regimens of treatment that involve application of knowledge, diagnosis, judgment.

I'm also impressed with the problem solving and troubleshooting that are integral to these occupations. The diesel program is built around it; after all, the mechanic's job kicks in when a vehicle malfunctions. "You're like a doctor," one of the students tells me. "You use all your senses, and you also ask the driver, what'd you hear? Feel? Smell? And you put that together." What caught my attention, though, was the degree of problem solving and troubleshooting in fashion. As we saw in several of the scenes from the sewing room, students are continually thinking back through what they did to correct something that didn't come out as they had imagined it.

This skill at problem solving is ultimately made possible by a quality I watched develop in all the trades I observed: the understanding of the human body, or a vehicle or a garment on a person as more than the sum of its parts, as a system. The choice of material and the design and stitching of the bodice can affect other areas of the dress and the way it hangs and moves. A symptom in one part of the body can be signaling a problem somewhere else. "We don't want a big repository of facts," the director of the nursing program tells me. "We want students to *think!*" "The textbook gives you the mechanisms," a diesel student explains, "their function and their purpose. But Mr. Franco, he gets us to see that when x fails, then y fails. Man, that's a whole different story."

Many students come into the occupational programs with subpar literacy and numeracy skills. In some cases, these are students who didn't like the traditional academic curriculum and didn't do so well in it. Some programs require a certain level of skill for incoming students or, as with nursing, a number of prerequisites.

And some of the programs at this college encourage students to take extra courses required to get the associate's degree—which includes English and mathematics. Some faculty incorporate writing and math instruction into their courses, and there are several experiments going on where an English or math course is linked to an occupational course so that students can develop their writing and mathematical ability through material that is relevant to them. And the work itself, in nursing, fashion, or diesel technology, affords all sorts of opportunities to further develop their skills.

A lot is being written these days about so-called "soft" job skills: responsibility and punctuality, the ability to communicate and cooperate, workmanship, persistence. They are typically distinguished from "cognitive" skills, meaning everything from literacy and numeracy to the kinds of skills we've been observing, the skills of the trade. The focus of discussion about "soft" skills is always on blue-collar and service workers, so there's a troubling social-class dimension to this discussion. After all, it's a truism in our culture that perseverance, commitment, caring about the quality of your work are among the fundamental qualities that also separate the superior athlete from the average, or the good architect or physician or banker from the not-so-good ones—but a discussion of the soft skills of white-collar workers hasn't become a topic of national discussion. Also, I'm not so sure that "cognitive" and "soft" skills are two distinct categories—or at least not as separable as is implied in policy discourse.

To be sure, students come into occupational programs with habits, past successes or failures, and personality characteristics that will affect their performance. But these qualities can also develop in and through the programs if the work grabs a student's attention and imagination. Whether as children or adults, we don't develop these qualities in a vacuum but through human interaction and meaningful activity. (A surefire way to fail to instill "soft skills" would be to talk about them in the abstract or to lecture students about them.) When our mind is engaged, when we can see ourselves learning how to do things, when we develop knowledge—then we also begin to care about what we do.

Ultimately, we're talking about identity, about our sense of who we are. When occupational programs are well conceived, those students who succeed in them are socialized into the values of the trade: workmanship, ethical practice, standards of excellence. These values might well get compromised in particular people's lives or in the marketplace, but students appropriate them and express them often in judging their own work and the work of others. What also happens is that students incorporate what they learn into their lives and begin to move through the world in a different way. I'm a nurse or a designer or a damned good mechanic. A student nurse told me about being at a park and a man nearby passed out. She automatically ran over to help the guy while someone called 911. She knew what to do and what questions to ask. "Oh my gosh," she thought later, "I really am a nurse."

III. Transferring to a University

"The wonder of it," is how William explains his fascination with astrophysics. "What's out there?" he asks softly but with emphasis. "What's really out there?" He knows he's got a long way to go, but he's getting closer with every semester. He's taking calculus now and Chemistry II; then next term it's more calculus and a physics course on the mechanisms of solids. "This is where my heart is." In a year, he plans to transfer to a university.

We're sitting at an old table in the back of his community college's tutoring center, where he works. He's in his mid-twenties, a lightweight boxer's build, jeans, a hoodie, quietly articulate. The origins of his interest in astrophysics lie not in science but in homelessness and his mother's desperation.

There was a time, he explains—he was seven or eight—when he, his younger brother, and mother lived in their car, then in an abandoned house. His mother worked three jobs, but she still couldn't make enough for rent. He would wake up in the middle of the night and find her crying, "turning to the sky and praying to God to 'Help us. Help us. Help us.' . . . And I would wonder 'Why is she looking to the sky? I know she says there's a God, but what's really out there?'"

He started doing well in his science courses in middle school and high school. But, according to him, the thing "in the end that really topped it off" was the Discovery Channel. William was "amazed" to learn about "all these people looking at the stars and sending robots out into space. So I started doing research on it, and I found out that it all had to do with physics."

It took years of working, being dissatisfied, taking one class, then another, changing jobs, learning the ins and outs of college, trying to balance work and school, trying the graveyard shift, starting a family, taking more classes, asking more questions. William finally got all the pieces together. "I kind of had to discover everything on my own, but now I'm not gonna let anything stop me."

The tutoring center is one large room with computer stations along two walls; there are also five round tables closer to us with computers on them. Two old couches sit side by side close to the entrance, and other tables—like the one William and I share—and chairs are spread around the room, some separated from the others with movable partitions. A lot goes on here. In addition to tutoring, the center hosts workshops on everything from using the computer to writing the college admissions essay. A sizable number of students on this campus do not own a computer, or they lack Internet access, so they come here as well to do assignments. And some students have grown attached to the center and stop in for quick advice on everything from course selection to problems with family life. There's a homey feel to the place. While I was interviewing William, an older woman was chatting with one of the tutors, urging her to get her flu shot, and a guy from the culinary program, white coat and chef's hat, came in bringing a tray of pastries.

In front of us, a tutor is helping a woman narrow down her topic for a psychology paper. "I'm trying to figure out how people become more tolerant." Over to our left, another tutor is sitting alongside a big man in a muscle T-shirt. "Give us some insight as to why you're using this quotation," she says, and he nods and leans into the keyboard. Alongside them, another tutor is encouraging a diminutive young woman; he cradles his head in his hand, looking at her sideways: "You do have some second-language writing issues, but your vocabulary is great." Then, "Don't let the frustration beat you. You'll get this."

I started coming to the tutoring center because the remedial classes I was observing required students to complete some online assignments there. I was impressed with the tutors, with their intelligence and camaraderie, and with their commitment to the work. They talked about "making a difference," about wanting to do more, about feeling "overwhelming gratitude" for the opportunity to be so involved in other people's lives.

The tutors were either preparing to transfer to a university or had already done so and kept their job at the center. I got to know them pretty well and, once my other work was completed, would increasingly stay late and talk with them.

Antonio did well in high school—he was the editor of his school's newspaper—and went straight to college but had to quit because of illness. He picked up again at a community college in another city, then came here and transferred last year to a local private university as an English major. He loves to talk about books and writing, about the way literature becomes part of you, the characters and plots becoming "engraved in you." He's reading Raymond Chandler and laughs as he explains how he'll be walking down the street and "the next thing I know I'm describing what I'm doing," in that distinct Philip Marlowe voice.

Larry is the tutor who, head in hand, was encouraging the young woman who wasn't a native speaker of English. He's in his mid-thirties, an ex-marine who was in and out of prison after his discharge, got his life together at this college, and is now a double-major at one of the state universities, in linguistics and conflict resolution. He says with amazement how much he loves what he's doing, given that he hated, just hated, high school. He's taking an African studies course, sociology of the family, labor studies, and a course in the psychology of peace building taught by a former United Nations negotiator. He tells me about his project: designing a charter school in the Occupied Territories for Arab and Israeli children.

Many years ago, I worked in a tutoring center at another community college and later went on to direct one at UCLA, so I have a soft spot for them, for the very idea of them: a common space where students come to learn things in a more personal way, to test their own understanding of material, to try out ideas, to practice a developing skill with the guidance of more-skillful others.

There's a lot to say about the center we've been visiting—the students it serves, the dedication of its tutors—but one thing that particularly strikes me is how frequently the current tutors were once receiving services here themselves. The same is true for the fellow who manages the center. He's now a graduate student in education at a nearby state university, but he began his postsecondary career at this campus after an injury made it impossible to continue working in the meat-processing industry. He placed into low-level math (pre-algebra) and equally low in English. He had a lot of remedial course work in front of him. But he came to the center, slowly made his way up the remedial ladder, took his general education requirements, transferred, got his BA, entered graduate school, and came back here to tutor, and then to help run the place. Within the little institutional niche of the tutoring center, there is both upward mobility and reciprocity, whereby members of this miniature community over time have the possibility to sit on both sides of the table. Maybe that's one reason they seem to have such understanding of the students they work with. "It's a different world if you go straight from high school to college," a tutor named Cassandra told me. "I *was* that student sitting across from me."

Cassandra is in her late twenties, has a bright, round face, and brown, wavy hair that fans out across her shoulders. She looks you right in the eye when she talks to you. Students come to the center requesting her. She is a skillful tutor, working with a wide range of students, from those needing help developing an essay to those who are just learning English and are struggling with their textbooks. If you watched her at work or met her—she sticks her hand straight out to shake yours with a firm grip—you'd be as surprised as I was to hear her story. She moves through the center with assurance. She's planning to get a graduate degree in psychology. She is passionate and articulate about her work, has a sensibility forged from her own difficult experience. She lays out the problems some of her students have—poor academic preparation, little money, prison records, tumultuous personal lives—but "I would hate for them to just wither away without realizing their full potential, to know what they're worth, how smart they really can be."

Like most of the tutors here, Cassandra's path to college was neither linear nor certain. She did enter college right after high school and took a number of classes, but she felt out of place and inadequate and eventually quit. For some time, it had been hard for her to concentrate on school. Her mother was chronically ill and her father was distant and demeaning. "I was always worried."

I have known many students like Cassandra; in fact, I in some ways was one myself. She never got into big trouble but drifted through her classes, undistinguished. Things were unstable at home, and she was consumed with worry and disengaged at school—a disengagement that some teachers took to be intransigence, or worse. Several teachers did try to intervene in a way that might have been well intentioned, telling her that she'd better get focused or she "wasn't going to amount to anything." But that kind of talk only wounded her all the more. The damage of tough love. She was caught in an awful spiral of insecurity and retreat, which was interpreted as disdain, which led to Cassandra's further marginalization.

For much of her academic life, Cassandra felt like an outcast, ignored, not very bright, going nowhere. She's worked since she was sixteen, through high school and through and after her first stint at college. Those jobs were increasingly unrewarding. "I was just lost."

One day a few years back, a friend of hers invited her along to a basic-skills math class at her college so that they could then hang out afterward—an utterly random act. Sitting in the math class, Cassandra began to think about school, how long it had been, how this didn't feel so bad. The next term, she signed up for a speech class, "just for my own growth. I had no intention of going full-time or transferring." Then next term, one more class, a philosophy class. Then one more term, one more class. Then one year after that serendipitous visit to math, she enrolled in an English composition class that "totally changed everything for me."

This professor wasn't easy; he'd challenge students, make them defend what they wrote or said. But according to Cassandra there was something about the way he looked at you while he was challenging you. "You knew he meant well." This professor called on the reluctant Cassandra, spoke to her in the hall about her papers, asked for her opinion about things, asked what she wanted to do with her life. "I never had a teacher talk to me like that. He was poking at my brain. 'Wow,' I thought, 'I'm not dumb!'"

While she was taking the professor's course, Cassandra was coming to the tutoring center, working regularly with two tutors. Toward the end of the term, one of them laid down his pencil, put his hands on the table and said flatly, "One of these days, you're gonna be sitting here tutoring somebody else." This was one more in a string of light-bulb moments Cassandra was having at the college. And she began to think, "I have to do this. I'm going to transfer."

———

One of the major goals of public and private initiatives aimed at the community college is to increase the rate of transfer to a four-year college or university. There are just over twelve hundred community colleges in the United States, and depending on their location and the demographics of the high schools and neighborhoods that feed into them, they have varied levels of success in fulfilling their transfer mission. Community colleges can provide services and programs to support transfer, and one strategy that helps is to create "learning communities," or "first-year experience programs," or programs built around "at risk" populations—

programs that create cohorts of students who take classes and receive services together.

In an informal way, this tutoring center functions as such a program. The management model encourages cooperation and shared responsibility among the tutors, and I frequently saw tutors conducting workshops together, sharing students, covering for each other. The tutors use their minds collectively in the service of others, creating in the process an intellectual community among themselves. Larry told me he considers the people in the center his family.

There are a lot of roads leading to a college degree, from the one straight out of high school to the retiree going back to school to complete a journey that was interrupted decades before. And there are many, many roads that lead to an intellectual pursuit, to physics or literature or psychology or the study of conflict and peace. The more varied the pathways to degrees and to intellectual pursuits—the more personal histories, the more points of view—the richer we are for it. Cassandra's experience in school and her work as a tutor will shape her study of the way people learn. Larry's life on the streets and in prison and the particular way he survived it all gives him a certain understanding of violence and reconciliation. And William's fascination with astrophysics has a heartbeat to it. Even if they end up asking the same kinds of questions that are asked by others in their courses, they will ask them in a different way.

FIVE

Overcoming Bad Ideas:

Toward Success with Remedial Education and Bridging the Academic-Vocational Divide

WHAT YOU SEE DEPENDS on where you sit, and for how long. You enter the classroom from the rear, wanting to be discreet on your first visit, and slip into the desk closest to the door. A few students notice you, but most are walking around or leaning over to the person next to them talking. Except for one woman, the class is all men in their twenties and thirties, a few White guys, the rest Black and Latino. Hoodies, baggy pants, loud profanity. The teacher is in front at a cloudy overhead projector. Three men are around him—each seems bigger than the next—and they are arguing.

The room is old and dingy, no windows, bare except for the irregular rows of desks, the table with the projector, a cart holding pipes and metal bars, and in the corner a worn flag from the American Welding Society. You're trying to take it all in when a sullen guy in an oversized t-shirt, a bandanna around his head, walks over to you and asks, "What are you doin' here?"

The classroom is attached to a large welding shop in a community college vocational program. Two days a week, the welding instructor teaches basic mathematics to his novice welders because some of them checked out of school long ago and never learned, or learned poorly, how to divide decimal fractions and calculate volume. And some knew it but have been away from it in the military or in a job that folded. Most people who make policy that affects students like these—and a fair number whose research involves them—haven't spent time in such classrooms. And, with few exceptions, those who do aren't there for long.

But if you stay. . . and come back. . . and come back again, you'll notice that on some days the baggy jeans and oversized tees are traded off for work shirts with company logos on the back. As you move around the room, you'll hear that amid the f-bombs, students are explaining to each other how to solve a problem or challenging someone else's explanation. The men walking over to other men's desks are typically bringing their open notebooks with them. The big to-do that can flair up around the projector—lots of pointing and trash talk—usually involves a disagreement among students about course work that they take right up to the instructor, the shadows of their fingers flitting across the diagrams on the overhead screen.

And that guy who wanted to know what you're doing here? Well, it's a legitimate question, isn't it? And everything depends on how you answer it. When it was posed to me, I said I was here to study programs like this one because we need to know more about them to convince our politicians that we need more of them. The man's features softened, and we moved out into the hallway. "We need programs like this," he said. "People like us." "It's the teacher that really makes a difference," he continued. "He treats us like we're people."

I later found out more about this man—his name is Ray. Ray has been in the two-year program for a year, is doing well and, in fact, just got a job. The boss sent the instructor an e-mail praising Ray, adding that he'd hire anyone else that good. The instructor then told me Ray's story. During his first few weeks in the program, he tried to cheat on a test of welding terms by erasing the name on a paper being handed toward the front and writing his name quickly across the top. This was so pathetic a move that several students called him on it—and, besides, the instructor could clearly see the traces of Ray's handiwork. Ready to throw Ray out of the program, the instructor called him into his office the next day, angry at both the stupidity and insult of Ray's stunt. Ray was mortified and begged to be given another chance. Ambivalent, uncertain, the instructor relented. "You just don't know," he said to me. "You have to be open in a program like this, give guys a chance to leave the streets behind." For the instructor, the program was a buffer zone. Some people will change. Some won't. It's hard to know in advance. But Ray seems to have made it.

For some time now, I have been studying cognition, language, and learning in low-status places—working-class schools, blue-collar job sites, adult schools, literacy programs, and remedial classrooms—places not privileged by society or, frequently, by the institutions in which they are located. Places like the basic math course and the welding program that houses it. I'm sure my interest in such places begins with my own history. My uncles were employed in the East Coast smokestack industries—railroad, automotive—and my mother was a waitress all her working life. That work kept us afloat, and seemed powerful. I loved watching it. As for school, I was an indifferent student, and once in high school, I spent two years going nowhere along a nonacademic track. A senior English teacher turned my life around—I tell that story elsewhere—and after struggling through a probationary first year of college, I began to find my way. So, all in all, I know the remedial side of the street pretty well.

I'm going to fast-forward through my undergraduate English major (that English teacher had turned me on to literature, and, besides, *he* was an English major) and zoom across a subsequent year of a doctoral program in English—which turned out to be too removed from the work of the world for me. Looking to ground myself and make a living, I found the Teacher Corps, a War on Poverty program that placed prospective teachers in low-income schools. That was my introduction to teaching and education, and after Teacher Corps I would go on to work for eight more years in a community college and in a range of programs for special populations: from traffic cops and parole aides to returning Vietnam veterans.

I see now how much the Veterans Program in particular shaped my subsequent teaching and development of curriculum—and eventually my research on remediation. The twelve-week program was developed by UCLA Extension and funded through the GI bill. It was housed in an old building in downtown Los Angeles, far away from UCLA itself. The purpose of the program was to prepare the vets for some level of postsecondary education. They took math, reading, speech, and writing courses and an introductory course in psychology that gave them transfer credit. This was my first job out of Teacher Corps, where I had taught language arts to children; now I was facing adults my age or older, and I wasn't sure what to do. But God looks out for drunks and fools, and I began to see that if this really was a *preparatory* program, then I could simulate for the vets the kind of intellectual tasks and writing assignments they would face in college.

I knew, for example, that they would have to systematically compare events or processes or texts. So I started them off with a few lines on human solidarity from John Donne and from the Caribbean poet and statesman Aimé Césaire, and over a few weeks we worked our way up to an astronomy-textbook account of the Big Bang and an Australian aboriginal myth about the origins of the cosmos. We would talk about these passages, look up words, puzzle together over what they meant and then list as precisely as we could similarities and differences in the content, in language, and who we imagined the audience for each to be. Then as best as they could, the veterans wrote out what they had discovered, sometimes in class as I went desk to desk, sometimes with the tutors the program hired—and when they were available, I'd bring one of the tutors into my classroom. Then the vets would revise their papers at home and come back for another round.

After all this work in special programs, I would go on to run the Educational Opportunity Program Tutorial Center at UCLA, a summer bridge program, and the Freshman Composition Program. Eventually, I and my colleagues in the tutorial center further developed the curriculum I started in the Veterans Program and fashioned another model for remediation in which we linked writing courses to introductory courses in political science, history, and psychology. This approach is in the air again today, used in college "learning communities" and in "contextualized learning"—for example, the way that welding teacher in the opening vignette teaches basic math in relation to an occupation.

In hindsight I realize how important it was that my first encounter with college remediation happened in the Veterans Program. It was both geographically and symbolically a far distance from UCLA. If we had been within the university's orbit, the prescribed curriculum for a remedial writing course would have been a grammar and punctuation workbook with some short readings—for that standard model for the college remedial writing course has been with us since the 1930s, was in place at UCLA in the late 1970s, and is quite present today. Let me sketch it out for you.

All community colleges and the majority of colleges and universities offer some form of remedial writing instruction. In the university, there is typically one remedial course; in the community college, three or four, taken in sequence.

Though there is variation—and some new developments that I'll discuss later—the standard remedial writing curriculum, especially as you move down the remedial ladder to the most basic course, includes a print or online workbook with grammar exercises ("Circle the correct pronoun in this sentence: *their* or *they're*" "Change the tense of the following verbs from present to past"). The workbook might also contain some short general-interest readings. The highest-level remedial course might have a separate reader arranged thematically (sections on work, school, family, coming of age) or perhaps a composition textbook, often with readings. Depending on the level, there will usually be some writing assignments, ranging from, at the lowest level, sentences and single paragraphs up to short papers (often the five-paragraph essay) on a topic related to one's personal experience or a current social issue. Most remedial writing textbooks emerge from and reinforce this standard model.

The first thing that probably strikes you about this curriculum is how familiar it is. The second thing, especially with the more basic courses, is how little it feels like college. A lot of students sense that, too.

Long-standing—and seemingly reasonable—assumptions about language and learning underlie this approach to writing instruction. And I heard them all once I moved to the tutorial center at UCLA and became acquainted with both the remedial textbook market and remedial programs at four- and two-year colleges up and down California.

Here in a nutshell is the rationale for the curriculum and for the lockstep sequence of courses. To teach a complex skill, especially if someone is having difficulty with it, you break the skill down into its constituent parts and have novices practice and practice them. In writing, fundamentals would be the rules of grammar and punctuation as represented in those workbook exercises. In addition to breaking down, you want to keep a tight focus on the task—writing—and remove potentially confounding variables, like reading skill. So if readings are used, they are usually kept simple and at a minimum. This parsing out of reading from writing is structurally reinforced in many institutions with reading and writing each having its own department. Another potentially confounding variable you want to control for is complexity of topic: what students write about if writing beyond the sentence is involved. The standard remedial playbook for decades and decades includes topics involving one's personal experience ("Write about an event that changed your life") or a broad social issue ("Why should we vote?"). Reinforcing these assumptions about writing and learning is an assumption about motivation. I would hear often that remedial writing students could be overwhelmed—which is true—and that therefore we need to keep assignments within a comfort zone and give students the experience of succeeding. All this forms a pretty tight web of assumptions, internally coherent, the common sense of remediation. Similar assumptions drive the standard approach to remediation in reading and mathematics.

But common sense wasn't always common; it begins somewhere. This atomistic skills orientation to learning originates in the simplified behaviorism of early American academic psychology—E.L. Thorndike and company. The remedial English class so familiar to us took shape during the first decades of the twentieth century when psychologists were studying language by reducing it to its discrete elements and defining growth as the accretion of these elements. The way to remedy error is to do studies that precisely determine common errors (for example, subject-verb agreement), and then develop exercises to build what those psychologists called "habit strength" in correct agreement. The workbook and "practice pad," new to the market at that time, provided the vehicle for such practice. Exercises in the workbooks of the 1920s are similar to the ones in workbooks and on computer screens today.

The problem is that we have over half-a-century's worth of research in linguistics, rhetorical and writing studies, cognitive and cultural psychology, and education that undercuts this approach and the aforementioned assumptions that support it. Language growth is much more complex—and this fact applies equally to native and nonnative speakers of a language. Isolated workbook or online exercises don't necessarily transfer to one's writing. Error in writing is not static; errors corrected in basic narrative can re-emerge in more complex exposition. To remove or reduce reading and to assign primarily personal or general opinion assignments does not prepare one to write for most of the other courses in the academic or vocational curriculum, courses most students are in at the same time they are taking remedial writing. And as for the claim that students' academic identity and motivation will benefit from unchallenging assignments—that's both unsubstantiated and patronizing. Finally, on the structural level, that sequence of courses has proven to be more of a barrier than an aid to college success; as I discussed earlier, a disheartening number of students never make it through the series to freshman English.

Complementing these reductive assumptions about learning is a second foundational influence on remediation, and when I was running the tutoring center and developing preparatory programs, I heard it frequently from administrators and faculty, English to biology, university to community college. Mixed with the language of discrete skills was a language that was essentially medical. Students in remedial classes had "handicaps," "disabilities," "defects," and "deficits" that had to be targeted and treated—almost as though their writing or math problems were organic and could be diagnosed and surgically removed. This vocabulary fits nicely with the atomistic approach to language and language growth. I also heard that students were in remedial courses because they were limited cognitively. They can't think clearly or logically or have trouble with abstraction or just aren't that smart. It's no surprise that a common name for the remedial writing course was Bonehead English. I still hear the term today.

Partly to counter claims that these students weren't intelligent and partly to generate theoretical explanations for their problems with writing, some people in writing and literary studies drew from contemporary theories about cognitive development and brain function and applied those theories to remedial writers. Perhaps flawed writing is caused by differences in cognitive style or in brain activity or from being arrested at an early stage of intellectual development or from growing up in a subculture that is more oral than literate. This is a kinder, gentler set of explanations than saying students are stupid, but it still posits fundamental differences in brain function and language use. Some of the vocabulary has changed, but remedial discourse is still full of loose talk about "learning styles" as well as about "handicaps" and "disabilities." This brew of organic and mental measurement language locates all causality within the individual and reduces and reifies problems with reading, writing, or mathematics.

As best as I can tell, this perspective on remediation has its origins in the first few decades of the twentieth century as medical doctors begin to work with children who today we would recognize as having a learning disability. But without knowledge of learning disabilities, the physicians analogized from the symptoms of adult stroke victims to explain the children's difficulties with language; somehow the otherwise healthy children were born with the language processing liabilities that in adults come from cerebral trauma. And as physicians began to pose more functional rather than trauma-based explanations and treatments for the children's difficulties, their language remained medical. One influential expert wrote of the "handicap" of these "physiological deviates."

As often happens with labels and categories, the remedial designation grew to include a wider and wider range of students, virtually anyone having difficulty in school, from those with poor vision or inadequate vocabulary to those who were just shy. Yet the medical cast remained. Here is a passage from a 1930 textbook on written examinations:

> Teaching bears a resemblance to the practice of medicine. Like a successful physician, the good teacher must be something of a diagnostician. The physician by means of general examinations singles out individuals whose physical defects require more thorough testing. He critically scrutinizes the special cases until he recognizes the specific troubles. After a careful diagnosis he is able to prescribe intelligently the best remedial or corrective measures.

It is telling that one of the nicknames during the 1930s for college-level remedial classes was "sick sections." In the 1940s it was "hospital sections." And, as I mentioned, there is the more recent appellation of "Bonehead English," not pathologic, perhaps, but calcified, organic, thick, and dense.

What happens to reading, writing, and mathematics in such

an environment? They become narrow, mechanical pursuits, stripped of fuller meaning. Students are tested, placed in courses, strive to fulfill requirements, are tested again, jump through another hoop. There's no denying that many students over the years have learned valuable things in these courses because of dedicated and inspiring teachers, but when you look at the broader picture you see how much effort is spent with limited gains. Students will define "good writing" as not making grammatical mistakes. To be proficient in mathematics you have to "memorize the rules." Grammar and algorithmic procedure are crucially important, but to define literacy and numeracy that way is like defining basketball as dribbling. Even introductory general education courses in political science or biology or astronomy are not taught in this fashion. A real grasp of literacy and numeracy doesn't seem to be the goal.

Consider as well the image of the person that is created by the medical discourse and the skills-and-drills approach to instruction. It is an image tinted with abnormality and stigma and conveys a pretty undynamic and unnuanced mental life. The image is also marked by social class and race. To be sure, a number of students from middle-class and well-to-do families are in remedial classes. When I was doing the work, I taught a fair number of them. But for all the reasons we know—from inadequate schooling to family disruptions stemming from housing, employment, health, or immigration status—low-income students are overrepresented in remedial classes, and, in some locations, these students are largely people of color. This is where that remedial language of handicaps and differences has further insidious ramifications, for we have a societal tendency to meld poor academic performance with cognitive generalizations about class and race—witness *The Bell Curve*, an attempt to explain the social order in terms of IQ.

Further issues of status and bias—both structural and symbolic—run throughout the remedial system. There is a status hierarchy of disciplines in higher education; not all courses are created equal—and the remedial course is in the lower depths. This inferior position is underscored by the fact that the courses for the most part do not carry credit, and credit is the institutional signifier of legitimacy. (Lack of credit also has economic consequences for students in terms of persistence, degree completion, and possible transfer.)

And, of course, there is not only a status hierarchy among disciplines but among postsecondary institutions as well, from elite research universities to the central-city community college. Though colleges and universities have had some type of remedial or preparatory course or program in their curriculum since the mid-nineteenth century, they have always been a source of vexation—and, at times, something akin to moral panic. We are seeing attempts in about twenty states now to reduce or remove remedial courses from the college and university, typically directing students to community colleges. Conversely, the open-access community college for much of its history has provided remedial or preparatory work as part of its mission, though the demand has increased as more people are attempting postsecondary education, and as state legislators and university administrators push remediation down the status ladder to the least resourced of our institutions of higher learning.

The people who teach remedial courses at the university or college level are almost always graduate students or adjunct instructors, and adjuncts are widely used at the community college level as well. These people have the least power among faculty. And because of the constraints on their role and time—and the fact that many adjuncts are rushing to two and three colleges to make a living—they typically don't have the time or training to rethink the remedial curriculum. (Some do, but it is a daunting task.) Thus those remedial textbook publishers who replicate the curriculum are, in part, responding to the market.

Although some who teach remedial classes, in the words of one community college department chair, "resent the students and feel they [the instructors] deserve better," it's been my experience that many of those who teach the courses put considerable effort into doing right by their students. But even if they resist it, they do that work within the remedial superstructure.

These interlayered dimensions of educational remediation—the curricular and ideological, the structural, and the symbolic—are a formidable barrier to change. Reformers might alter something structural, but the assumptions underlying the curriculum remain the same. Or instructors might create new curricula but can't simultaneously work on the structural level. Comprehensive change begins to feel remote.

But, in fact, remedial education has worked for some students, powerfully so. And there is a long history—unfortunately not well known in larger policy circles—of teachers working against the grain and developing educationally rich curricula and programs. I can say without reservation that basic-skills work represents as rich an area of study and as intellectually engaging an arena of teaching as you'll find. If adults are having trouble with fractions, for example, how did their misunderstandings and flawed procedures develop? What formal or informal mathematical knowledge do they have that can be tapped? How does one access that cognitive history and lead students to analyze and remedy it? How, then, does one proceed to teach in a way appropriate to adults with that history? Suddenly we are dealing not only with a challenging instructional problem but also with a number of fascinating issues in mathematics education, cognitive science, the philosophy of mind, and social theory.

Furthermore, basic-skills instruction, when done well, requires a serious consideration of disciplinary basics that tend to be taken for granted. In teaching remedial writing, I have found myself thinking about and trying to explain the origins and purpose of the conventions of literacy—grammar and punctuation and written forms such as the list, the chart, and the narrative. And there's the connection between the solitary act of writing and an audience, the complex relationship between speech and writing; and the habits of mind, the intellectual strategies I taught to the veterans. But we don't appreciate the intellectual content of the work because of professional and institutional bias.

We are at a propitious time when public and philanthropic resources are focused on remedial education, and a lot of smart people are experimenting with new curricula, online learning, and altering those restrictive course sequences. The crucial questions facing us are: how will we define the students in remedial education, and what kind of education will we envision for them?

Let's go back to those novice welders we met earlier. Along with the basic math class, the instructor teaches the students how to read blueprints, and often the math and blueprint reading blend together. Among other materials, the instructor uses the blueprints from a recent campus construction project, and the prints sometimes bear numbers or notes scribbled by the architect or contractor. This blueprint work provides the occasion for some pretty impressive reasoning. The students have to know the function of different kinds of welds and whether or not a weld would be appropriate in a particular place represented on the blueprint. They have to visualize a structure from the blueprint and perform various mental operations on it: how will multiple pieces fit together? What happens to them when you weld them? The arithmetic they're learning or reviewing is materialized in an actual building, and they have to imagine arithmetic in three-dimensional space to make judgments and solve problems. In these moments, basic math isn't so basic.

Every once in a while, the notations added by the architect and contractor will be unclear or, worse, there will be a discrepancy between them. These situations reveal the ability of some of the students to apply what they know to an ambiguous problem.

After math, after blueprints, the cohort of students join other cohorts out in the large welding workshop. It is loud with grinders, hammering, metal falling to the floor, and people yelling over it all. There is the sharp odor of chemicals and electricity, especially as you get close to the work stations, and bursts of sparks and intense light all across the room.

When you talk to students after a weld, you get a sense of their developing knowledge of electricity and metals and the pros and cons of different welding processes. The instructor, who travels among them—checking in, giving quick demonstrations—helps them use this knowledge to figure out how a weld went wrong. In addition to their technical chops, they're developing an aesthetic sense of the work—they talk about a "beautiful" weld—and an understanding of the relationship of aesthetics and function. And they're developing an ethics of practice; a bad weld can have big consequences. "A bridge is only as strong as its weakest weld," the other instructor in the room tells her students. "You're taking two separate entities and making them one. You're like a surgeon, but you're working on metal. So take it to heart."

One of the abilities the students develop is particularly fascinating to me, and that is the intricate interplay between kinesthetics and thought. Around the perimeter of the workshop are small cubicles that shelter the main room from blinding light and also enable students to practice certain kinds of welds. Tommy steps out from one of them, sees me, flips up his mask, and slips off his right leather glove to shake hands—his is warm and damp from the heat. He's one of the second-semester students from the math class. I ask him what he's working on in there, and, with increasing animation, he explains and demonstrates how he's practicing his vertical and overhead techniques. I say I can't imagine welding overhead, and he laughs, "Overhead is something else!"

The central precepts of welding are travel—the speed at which you move the instrument—the distance of the instrument from the metal, the angle of it, and how hot you've got it. And you have to be steady. Tommy puts one foot in front of the other and raises his right hand, forefinger out like a welding tool. He braces himself, though he can't be rigid, for that will impede the fluidity of his movement.

Travel, angle, and all that are further complicated in some processes by the fact that the electrode conducting the current is being used up as you weld, so you've got to continually adjust your travel speed and angle and distance to keep things constant—for consistency is crucial to producing a good weld. And you're doing all this over your head. Tommy relaxes his stance and looks at me. "There's so much you need to know," he says, tapping his forehead. "So much to think about."

Tommy is engaged in intense self-monitoring and analysis of his performance and significant intellectual work in applying what he's been learning to the task in front of him. It's hard to know where to mark the Cartesian separation between body and mind. Touch and concept blend in activity. Of course, as Tommy masters his trade, his response to the dynamic variability he describes will become second nature. We typically use words like "routine" or "automatic" to describe this level of expertise, but I think that vocabulary erroneously suggests that at a point in development, mind fades from physical performance. It's true that constant monitoring does diminish, but not mindfulness and not that fusion of touch and concept, as you'll see in welding or hairstyling or heart surgery when something goes wrong. Suddenly attention is focused, and all kinds of knowledge rush in on the moment, right through the fingertips.

This is the kind of thing that captivated me for the six years I spent researching the cognition involved in blue-collar and service occupations. There's a level and variety of mental activity involved in doing physical work that is largely unacknowledged, even invisible—especially in our high-tech era. This diminishment of occupational cognition bears directly on big issues in education: the decades-long effort to reform Career and Technical Education, the college-for-all debate, and the current initiatives to get more low-income people into and through postsecondary certificate or degree programs. These laudable efforts occur on a centuries-old landscape marked by the sharp divide I discussed in "Full Cognitive Throttle" between the academic and the vocational courses of study. I want to consider this divide more fully here, for I think it narrows our understanding of human cognition and straitjackets our pedagogical imagination.

As we saw with remediation, this issue has curricular-ideological, structural, and symbolic dimensions that are tightly interconnected.

The foundation for a status-laden and cognitively inflected distinction among kinds of work goes quite far back in Western thought. In *The Republic* Plato notes that the soul of the craftsman is "warped and maimed," and in his *Politics* Aristotle proposes that artisans and merchants be denied citizenship because their work is "ignoble and inimical to goodness." Though Western intellectual history includes many dissenting voices, from St. Augustine to our own John Dewey, the pervasiveness of this perspective is striking. It certainly runs through America's cultural history—

odd in a country with an anti-intellectual streak and such a strong orientation toward practicality.

Looking back over our history, labor journalist John Hoerr observes: "Since the early days of industrialization, a peculiar notion has gained ascendancy in the United States: that wage workers . . . lacked the competence to handle complex issues and problems that required abstract knowledge and analytical ability." This tendency was evident when post–Revolutionary War mechanics were portrayed in editorials as illiterate and incapable of participating in government, and it was alive and well when an auto industry supervisor told me that his workers were "a bunch of dummies."

This set of beliefs and distinctions about knowledge, work, and the social order affects the structure of educational institutions in the United States. At the postsecondary level, as historian Laurence Veysey observes, a tension going back to the mid-nineteenth century exists between liberal study and what he calls utility. Is the goal of education to immerse students in the sciences and humanities for the students' intellectual growth and edification or to prepare them for occupation and public service? With the increase in vocationally oriented majors since the 1960s, the utilitarian function is clearly in ascendance. Yet you don't have to work in a college or university very long to sense the status distinctions among disciplines, with those in the liberal tradition, those seen as intellectually "pure" pursuits—mathematics, philosophy—having more symbolic weight than business, nursing, or education. As I said earlier, not all courses are created equal.

Vocational education at the secondary level took shape in the first decades of the twentieth century with the development of the comprehensive high school and curriculum tracking. This new kind of school was in large part a response to the rapid increase of working class and immigrant children in urban centers, and tracking seemed an efficient way to address their wide range of educational preparation and ability.

But conceptions of ability were made within the legacy that journalist John Hoerr summarizes, and amid the emergence of IQ testing and a full-blown eugenics movement. There was much talk about the limited mental capacity of various immigrant and working-class groups and the distinct ways their brains functioned. As opposed to college-bound students (overwhelmingly White and middle to upper class) who were "abstract minded," working-class and immigrant students were "manually minded." So there again is the tight chain-link of cognition-education-work-and-social class.

This approach to education had an effect on vocational education itself. Almost from its inception, voc ed has been criticized for focusing too narrowly on job training and for not intellectually challenging its students. Exceptions to this portrayal of vocational education certainly exist, both teachers and programs, secondary and postsecondary, where students got an intellectually demanding education. And, although not typically mentioned in this regard, there is a separate history of worker education programs that blend politics, social sciences, and humanities with occupational education, from early-twentieth-century labor colleges to contemporary institutions like the Van Arsdale Labor Center at Empire State College.

A focused national attempt to enhance vocational education in our time came with the Carl D. Perkins Vocational Education and Technology Act of 1990 which, among other things, funded attempts to increase the academic content of vocational education. The results over the years, as is the case with any reform, have been varied, ranging from the superficial (slapping a prepackaged math module onto a course in business or health care) to the substantial: members of both the academic and the vocational faculty working for months to develop a curriculum that integrates academic and vocational material. And in a few cases, a visionary faculty in places such as Hi Tech High and Big Picture Schools used voc ed reform as the occasion to reimagine the very structure of schooling itself and with it the academic-vocational divide. They develop curricula that merge rather than reinforce disciplines and find in the occupational world rich educational content.

This kind of innovation is hard to achieve, however, for as with remediation, we retain a tight cluster of culturally transmitted assumptions about cognition, knowledge, academic achievement, and social class that constricts our educational creativity. The way subject areas and disciplines are organized in school contributes to the problem. Future teachers come to view knowledge in bounded and status-laden ways. There is no place in, let's say, a historian's training where she is assisted in talking across disciplines with a biologist, let alone to a person in medical technology or the construction trades.

These separations are powerfully reinforced when people join an institution. The academic-vocational divide has resulted in separate departments, separate faculty, separate budgets, separate turf and power dynamics. Now egos and paychecks enter the mix. These multiple separations lead to all sorts of political tensions and self-protective behaviors that work against curricular integration. It certainly doesn't help that efforts at integration are often framed such that the academic side will bring the intellectual heft to the vocational courses, a laying on of culture. In line with the history I have sketched, the cognitive content of occupations is given short shrift.

But as with remedial education, this is a promising moment. All those Perkins-initiated reforms of the last few decades have yielded some terrific programs and ideas. The notion of contextualized learning is getting wide attention. And public and private resources are being directed toward workforce development for the new economy. As with attempts at reform of remediation, the big question is: What kind of education will all this yield?

———————

Let me close with several observations. When I was teaching remedial English, one of my primary goals was to change the model of writing my students carried in their heads. Over our time together, I wanted them to begin to conceive of writing as a way to think something through and give order to those thoughts. I wanted them to understand writing as persuasion, to get the feel for writing *to* someone, a feel for audience. And I wanted them to revise their writing process, which for most of them was a one-draft affair typically done the night before or the morning an assignment was due. Though I paid a lot of attention to grammar and punctuation, I wanted them to see that good writing was more than correct writing. After years of basic-skills-oriented instruction, correctness—which is harder than hell to achieve if writing isn't meaningful to you—became their elusive holy grail.

That welding instructor will be the first to tell you that he doesn't know math very well. The ideal, he believes, would be to have a math teacher demonstrating the division of decimal fractions and calculation of volume, and explaining the *why* of what the class is doing, the mathematical principles involved. But what the welding instructor does do in that dingy little room adjacent to the welding workshop is bridge the academic-vocational divide and thereby redefine for his students the meaning and function of mathematics.

I began this chapter by suggesting that what you see depends on where you sit and for how long. Most higher education policy research on remediation and on Career and Technical Education does not include historical analysis of the beliefs about cognition and instruction that determine how students are taught. In fact, there's not a lot of close analysis of what goes on in classrooms, the cognitive give and take of instruction and what students make of it. We don't get much of a sense of the texture of students' lives, the terrible economic instability of some of them, but even less of a sense of the power of learning new things, and through that learning redefining who you are. Student portraits, when we do get them, are too often profiles of failure rather than of people with dynamic mental lives.

One reason for this state of affairs is that most of us in higher education are trained and live our professional lives in disciplinary silos. There may be no way around that in this day and age, but the least we can do is pull in more people from other silos and lock ourselves together in a room with pen and paper—and iPads, too. Let me give you one example of how mind-boggling, and, I think, harmful, this intellectual isolation can become. In all the articles I've read on remediation in higher education journals not one mentions the forty years worth of work on remedial or basic writing produced by teachers and researchers of writing. There is even a *Journal of Basic Writing* that emerged out of the open admissions policy at City University of New York in the 1970s. Not one mention. Zip.

Methodological silos also prevent the sharing of knowledge. Because no studies with randomized control experiments have appeared in the *Journal of Basic Writing*, some researchers dismiss the journal. This is not the place to go into the epistemological narrowness that ensues—you can read the best of research methodologists like Donald Campbell and Lee Cronbach on that topic—but I do want to suggest that if we hope to really do something transformational with remediation and with the academic-vocational divide, we'll need all the wisdom we can garner, from multiple disciplines and multiple methodologies, from multiple lines of sight.

As I've said, we are at a promising moment, what with all the attention and funding, public and private, focused on remediation and occupational education. But we are also at a crossroads, and it's a terribly consequential one. The probable road, given the way these things go, will lead to some worthwhile changes—shortened course sequences, for example, or better data collection on students in those courses. But the standard model of remediation or the divide between the vocational and the academic course of study will remain unchanged. So, to pick one illustration that is already emerging, we will have the development of more precise computerized tests of basic skills along with technically sophisticated modules aligned with those tests. As Bill Gates said during a recent radio interview, we will pinpoint what a student has trouble with and then "drill in" on that skill. This approach—and note his language—doesn't change the mechanistic theory of learning underlying such a program and doesn't represent a robust notion of literacy or numeracy. Mr. Gates didn't revolutionize the computer industry by making modest changes to existing technology. He rethought it. He and all of us need to think creatively and generously about the way we use electronic technology in remediation, for such technology is quickly being cast as the magic bullet of basic skills.

The other road, the one I've been taking us down, is possible right now, though it will require us to draw on more kinds of knowledge and more research methods than we typically use. This broader set of maps and instruments would enable us to consider simultaneously the curricular-ideological, the structural-economic, and the social class and symbolic dimensions of remediation and the academic-vocational divide.

But we will need one more thing. To truly seize the moment we will need a bountiful philosophy of education—and the leadership to enact it. At the same time that policy makers are trying to get more low-income people into postsecondary education, colleges are forced to limit enrollments and cut classes and student services. In my state of California (and in other states as well) some policy makers are raising the possibility that we can no longer afford to educate everybody, that we should ration our resources, directing them toward those who are already better prepared for college. We have here the makings in education of a distinction that historian Michael Katz notes in the discourse on poverty, a distinction between those deserving and undeserving of assistance. Enter once again the not-so-hidden injuries of social class blended with the stigma of underpreparation. In the midst of a powerful anti-welfare-state, austerity climate, will we have the political courage to stand against the rationing of educational opportunity?

The democratic philosophy I envision would affirm the ability of the common person. It would guide us to see in basic-skills instruction the rich possibility for developing literacy and numeracy and for realizing the promise of a second-chance society. It would honor multiple kinds of knowledge and advance the humanistic, aesthetic, and ethical dimensions of an occupational education.

The de facto philosophy of education we do have is a strictly economic one. This is dangerous, for without a civic and moral core it could easily lead to a snazzy twenty-first-century version of an old and shameful pattern in American education: working-class people get a functional education geared only toward the world of work. To be sure, the people who are the focus of current college initiatives are going to school to improve their economic prospects. As one woman put it so well: "It's a terrible thing to not have any money." But people also go to college to feel their minds working and learn new things, to help their kids, to feel competent, to remedy a poor education, to redefine who they are, to start over. You won't hear any of this in the national talk about postsecondary access and success. For all the hope and opportunity they represent, our initiatives lack the imagination and heartbeat that transform institutions and foster the wondrous, unrealized abilities of the full range of our citizenry.

SIX

Improving the People's College

ONE OF THE GREAT achievements of American higher education, an achievement uniquely ours, is its continued drive—not without conflict and contradiction—toward wider and wider inclusion. The community college has been especially valuable here, for over time it has achieved a remarkable level of access, open to all, often called "the people's college." What has become increasingly clear over the past few decades, however, is that access is a necessary but not a sufficient condition for achieving a robust and democratic system of higher education. It is not enough to let people in the door; we have to create the conditions for them to thrive once inside. For what they—what we—encounter is not always hospitable, and doesn't help us find our way and settle in. . . .

I can't find the right building, and, after difficulty parking, I am running late for a meeting with the dean. I've been on this campus before and have been on countless other college campuses over the years. College is familiar territory.

The dean I am looking for is in one of two large, newly constructed buildings, side by side, similar in design. One houses administration, student services, meeting rooms, and classrooms. The other building has classrooms, faculty offices, and some other administrative and staff offices. I left the dean's room number in the car, but no problem, I'll find him.

There are no prominent signs indicating which building is which. The main entrance to the first one I approach is closed. I find a side door. A video screen by the elevators is running an announcement on the college's health care programs. But there is no office directory. I go back outside and across the narrow lawn to the other building, which is open, but also has no directory. Out again to the lawn where I spot a security guard who tells me that the first building I was in houses the administrators. OK. Once again to that side door. I figure deans could be on the top floor, so I take the elevator up and walk the halls looking for the dean's name. But the offices are labeled by department, some of which sound similar (Occupational Education, Workforce Development), but none lists people's names. I start to enter one to inquire, when I see a woman I recognize as one of the vice presidents. She says it's easier to show me and walks me down two flights of stairs to another floor and to the right office—one without the dean's name on it.

I tell the dean about my adventure. He tells me that he was walking to a meeting on the first day of classes and was stopped "at least a dozen times" by students seeking directions. It was then that he noticed—he's new to the college—that there are no centrally located campus maps or directories.

After my meeting, going down the elevator, a woman with a large tattoo of a dragon on her arm gets on, stands silently for a moment, then turns to me furrowing her brow and asks, "Is this the floor for financial aid?"

Though this little story directly concerns signage and information, it is representative of a much larger cluster of issues: the accessibility and responsiveness of the interconnected components of college life: physical design, student services and activities, curriculum, and teaching.

Any student entering college is going to feel some mix of apprehension and excitement and is going to be thrown by unfamiliar landscape and routines. It wasn't my first time on the campus, and I *still* had problems making my appointment.

But if college itself is unfamiliar to you and if there is not in your family a collective history of experience with postsecondary institutions—well, then, the first days on a campus can be anxious, even disorienting. And, as with many of the students in this book, if school conjures up more negative than positive feelings, you can easily begin to doubt that you belong. I can't tell you how many students have used those words in characterizing their presence on a college campus: I'm not sure I belong here. On top of all this, imagine you're older and have a lot on your plate, problems with housing, supporting your kids, debt crashing in on you. Your tolerance for uncertainty and frustration is low, and that frustration mixed with self-doubt about your ability to handle college can make you turn away in anger.

Sam is a student I've gotten to know well. He's successful, involved in student government, works on campus. He feels at home here. He tells me about trying to get an appointment with a counselor to verify the credits he's got and the courses yet to take to be eligible to transfer to a four-year college. He goes to the primary reception area for appointments where a student worker tells him coldly that there are no more appointments available. None? No, none. End of story. Sam asks if there's someone further he can talk to. The worker says to go to the third floor, which Sam does. A second student worker there says the person Sam needs is not in. Sam asks if he can please get her contact information—Sam's learned the norms of institutional behavior—and the guy slides a pen over to him. Sam picks it up, ready to write what the guy says. Silence. Well, Sam asks . . . and the guy points to a phone number on the pen. Sam steels himself, writes the number down, and leaves. When Sam tells me the story we both imagine what would have happened if Sam had been a new student. How would he have reacted to the stonewalling disrespect? Would he have taken the guy's head off, or would he have silently walked away and possibly not come back?

A lot of attention is currently being paid to student development and success in college, and, over the years, I've written about these issues myself. Let me pull together some of the ideas in the air about making postsecondary education more responsive in order to increase the likelihood that students who have not had an easy time of it will do well. This is only a partial list, meant to illustrate broad themes. Much of what I'll discuss can also be fruitfully applied to all postsecondary settings, for even those students who are well prepared can find themselves discovering gaps in their education, confused by institutional norms and expectations, anxious about new challenges, and confronting a curriculum that is fragmented and pedagogically unsound. By looking closely at the problems of underprepared students, we can gain insight into the problems of higher education itself.

The Physical Environment

A college's architecture and landscape are both functional and symbolic. The design of buildings, the arrangement of offices and classrooms, the flow of traffic, the ease of access, the presence of common spaces—all these have a significant effect on what students do and how they feel about it. And all these features convey a host of messages about the identity and status of the campus and the nature of the educational experience it offers. Colleges that can afford to, devote considerable effort to creating a particular environment and use that environment—and images of it—in marketing their institution.

Many of the institutions that are the focus of this book do not have the kinds of resources that support large-scale construction or renovation projects or lush landscaping and aesthetic refinements. But the basic principle still holds: The built environment both constrains and enhances student experience. So upkeep and maintenance, routine landscaping, custodial and sanitation services all matter immensely. The condition of bathrooms tells students a whole lot about how students are valued.

Within an institution's budgetary constraints, are there inviting common spaces? Places to read and study? Are classrooms set up in ways that encourage interaction? Are there signs and maps to help people get around? Are offices with similar or interrelated functions close to each other? On several campuses I've visited, all student services related to instruction are side by side in one building: a computer lab, writing center, math and science center, reading center. Access and ease of use are maximized, and staff from one center can walk students over to another center. A further telling thing is that although the buildings are old and worn from weather and use, the lab and centers are clean, organized, and run with friendly efficiency. The aesthetics of the settings aren't so hot, but everything else about them is inviting and signals *assistance*. Of course, money is important in making the physical environment a contributing factor to students' well-being. But what matters more is an understanding, a way of seeing the physical environment in terms of student need.

On that campus where I had my circuitous journey to the dean's office, the building that housed the library was being renovated, so the library was temporarily relocated. The library staff printed a bunch of 10 × 12-inch signs on a computer and taped, stapled, and hung them around the campus at regular intervals from the old location to the new. No matter where you were on campus, you could follow these signs and end up at the books. Someone should have been thinking that way at the campus level. So often when issues involving design and access come up, we rush to expensive consultants, work out grand plans of human-built environment interaction. But sometimes all we need is the equivalent of printed signs with arrows—and the understanding that generates them, the ability to see the campus through the eyes of the people the campus serves.

First Encounters

The physical layout of a campus has a significant effect on student well-being, but the human landscape is even more important, particularly the quality of the initial interactions one has with various campus services and resources. How do campus representatives—counselors, clerks, custodians—respond to questions? How helpful are they, and how do they treat us? Yes, Sam, the guy trying to see someone to verify his transfer credits, was given the information he was seeking: the contact number for the counselor. But he was treated in a terribly disrespectful way. I've had more than a few students tell me they wouldn't go back to an office or department because someone there so offended them. They resist, even when it is to their significant disadvantage to do so; for example, a young woman barely scraping by on a small settlement from a car accident refused to return to the financial aid office because her previous visits were so exasperating. What happens to students during their first semester is crucial to their persistence and success.

A common way in which this issue of service is addressed these days is with the language of commerce. Students are customers, and the college needs to be focused on their satisfaction. This way of framing the problem is probably inevitable in a business-oriented, managerial society such as ours, and it certainly does drive home the point. But let me also suggest other ways to frame the issue of responding to student needs. Some educators pose a human development model as a way to get us to direct student services and teaching more toward student growth. And I've wondered why we don't take a communitarian approach to these issues: that it is in the nature of a healthy community— taking the college as a small community—to foster growth and look out for all its participants equally, particularly the most vulnerable.

The student worker who slid that pen over to Sam wouldn't last long in the service industry, and his behavior, at the least, suggests that the people in his position should be better trained. But I wonder whether training in providing better customer service alone will do it. What we're talking about is an entire orientation toward students, an institutional philosophy that has a moral as well as consumerist dimension to it. Let me elaborate this point with two first-encounter examples: the front desk and student orientation.

The Front Desk. I was recently at a conference on increasing student success where some participants were discussing the crucial role of the front desk, the first point of contact. We typically see the front desk as a place to check in or to get preliminary information or as a routing point. But the front desk could be so much more. It is the entryway to campus resources, and during the first weeks of school, it opens or closes the door to fuller participation in campus services and campus life. Training to work at the front desk needs to be framed in this way, a job of considerable ethical and social, as well as administrative responsibility.

Because the quality of information delivered at the front desk is equally important to the quality of the interaction, extra staff— including counselors, advisers, and supervisors—could be assigned to the area, at least during the busy first few weeks of the term. Frontline workers could consult with these specialists, and many questions could be authoritatively answered on the spot. This arrangement could also increase the accuracy of referral information. If you're already a bit out at sea, it can be pretty frustrating to be sent to the wrong office.

The effectiveness of referrals could be greatly enhanced if the staff at the front desk were able to send a message ahead alerting the office on the other end. Current electronic systems make this possible, and tightening the referral loop would be of special benefit to those students who aren't used to having institutions respond to them in an efficiently helpful way.

These days, a good deal of the information students seek is available online, so the campus website becomes a virtual front desk. Seeing the site as a front desk brings to the fore a whole host of design issues that are beyond the scope of this discussion but that in general would be driven by the requirement that the site's content and design are matched to student need—which means expending some effort to understand that need before putting fancy technical systems in place.

The digital divide is still very much with us, so the ideal front desk area would also have computer terminals nearby. And because some students will not be familiar with navigating a website, terminals should be placed at the front desk itself, where staff can demonstrate when necessary how to find the information a student requires. As information systems get more advanced, this basic principle of assistance and demonstration will still hold.

Orientation. Every campus has some kind of activity—or set of activities—to provide an orientation to the campus, its mission, services, curriculum, and routines. Some of this is now done online. Orientations range from campus tours to welcoming speeches by campus officials to comprehensive presentations and workshops that extend for days. Some orientations are superficial and not very helpful, especially for first-generation college students, and some are extensive and smartly executed. I want to discuss briefly one exemplary program I attended that both provided information and invited participants into campus life.

This orientation was a three-day affair that involved slides, PowerPoint presentations, film clips, music, and guest speakers and was information-rich and inclusive. The big topics were covered, of course—registration, matriculation, and financial aid— but so were a wide range of student services for veterans, single parents, students with disabilities, and for those needing help with writing, reading, and mathematics.

Because a high percentage of new students at this college are academically underprepared, the presenters provided a lot of information on remedial courses in math and English and on the placement test aligned with them. Included in this discussion was information on getting a GED certificate. The presenters illustrated everything they discussed with examples from campus documents and online sites, and they encouraged questions to guide them. In talking to students during breaks, I could see that there was a degree of information overload here, but most got the big ideas and, at the least, knew that they would have to check on some topics further—and now they knew what those topics were. The architects of the orientation also created a one-unit class that students could take once they were in the thick of the semester, and this class provided a further opportunity to learn about college life and their place in it.

In addition to providing information, the presenters spent a fair amount of time talking about the intellectual and emotional benefits of the journey students were about to begin. These segments, which were woven throughout the three days, were a mix of stories (both drawn from the presenters' lives and the lives of their students, past and present), film clips and poems, strategies for reading and writing analytically, and near-sermonic appeals to embrace the intellectual and social resources of the campus: to go to faculty office hours and tutoring centers, to read, to take a class in something new, to drop your guard and meet other students. So along with all the strategic talk about the system of courses and placement tests and financial aid came a good dose of passion about the exploration that lay ahead.

Perhaps the single thing that most caught my attention was the way the speakers managed casually to include in their presentation people with backgrounds that are so often stigmatized: people with no high school diploma or with a prison record or who are undocumented, learning disabled, gay or lesbian, or immigrant. They did this with no fanfare, sometimes with humor, always with a light touch, like it ain't no big thing because we're all in this together now. So, for example, when discussing ways to get a GED certificate, they mentioned some people in their own families who took the GED exam and joked about the advantages of missing all those embarrassments and growing pains in high school—and still finishing school with an equivalency test. There were a lot of people in this college's population who had difficult backgrounds, and the presenters made them feel welcome, included, a natural part of the mix of students beginning this new phase of their lives.

Counseling and Information

"We are flying in the dark," the vice president says, throwing up her hands. She's referring to the lack of information on her campus about individual student behavior: classes taken, classes dropped, success rates of subpopulations of students. The campus has aggregate information—for example, how many students pass or fail basic-skills courses—but not information on individual students that could be used in a helpful way right here and now. "A bell should go off when a student drops a class," she says, slapping her hands back onto her desk.

There is a big drive at all levels of education to improve the collection of information on students, and at the college level the interest is in graduation rates, the success rates of at-risk populations, the rates of completion of courses—especially of what are called "benchmark" or "milestone" courses, such as basic-skills requirements or transfer-level English and mathematics. One sure way to get the attention of both government and philanthropic funders is to talk about information.

There is an equally strong desire to develop the means to provide better information to students about their records, where they stand in terms of particular benchmarks and goals, the courses they need to take, and how long it will take them to complete their goals, given where they are now. There is also discussion about how to use new electronic technology to assist in delivering this information: text messages, cell phone applications, and so on.

This focus on information directly relates to another timely issue in postsecondary education, and that is counseling and advising. We're all familiar with the reigning model of college counseling: students make appointments with professionals who can provide advice about course requirements, about one's progress, about alternative majors if one is interested, or, in another realm, about financial aid requirements and opportunities. Sam, whom we met earlier, was trying to see a counselor regarding transfer to a four-year college. Under the best of circumstances, counselors and advisers have very large student loads, and on average the students on the campuses we've been discussing come with the *least* specific knowledge about college requirements and bureaucratic routines. "I didn't even know what questions to ask," as one young woman put it. It is especially on such campuses that the traditional counseling model seems inadequate to the task. Some institutions are trying to distribute more advising responsibility to faculty—not at all easy when so many faculty are part-timers. And some colleges are assigning counselors to particular programs, so that, for example, one counselor deals with construction trades in the construction trades building. This arrangement enables the counselor to develop expertise and provides more and better access to services for the students.

As I noted, colleges are searching for more high-tech means to provide students with the information they need. If that virtual bell went off when a student drops a class, as the vice president desired, then a text could go out to the student inquiring as to the reason, and further information on options could follow. Understandably, given the revolution in communications and social media, a lot of people are looking to technology to solve the counseling problem.

There's no doubt about the benefits of getting better information about students and developing ways to provide information "just in time" as they are in the middle of decisions about courses, career goals, financial aid. I'm currently involved in some projects related to these efforts. But what I would hate to see is the elevation of information delivery over all other concerns involving counseling and advising. One of the surest findings in decades and decades of work in communications and in social psychology is that information doesn't just flow and get processed in a vacuum. Information flow is embedded in human interaction and social networks. We distribute information through each other and judge its merits based on who relays it to us.

One morning before the start of that orientation I visited, a young woman recognized me from the previous day's session and walked over, asking if she could talk to me. Stylish, deep red lipstick, sharp eyebrows, she was entering the cosmetology program. She held up several sheets of paper listing requirements for the program and additional courses to get an associate of arts degree. She started talking to me about the requirements, slipping in and out of a smile that registered both appreciation and bewilderment. In fact, she had a good grasp of the requirements, and as she talked her way through them, and I assented and explained a little more, she relaxed, the bewilderment fading. Maybe she just needed to hear herself articulate what was on paper; maybe she needed someone who looked like he might be on staff to confirm what she read. In any case, the information on her program—information she understood—got elaborated, or legitimized, or came alive as she talked her way through it with another person.

Teaching

With few exceptions, most graduate programs do not put much effort into helping people learn how to teach. Students master the central texts or exemplary studies of political science or physics, the discipline's methods of inquiry, the history of the discipline's development, but not how to teach it. Graduate students might assist in courses and learn that way, and they might pay special attention to how their professors teach, but none of this is systematic or a focus of study or mentoring. And there is no place in their curriculum where they consider the difficulties young people might have as they learn how to think like a political scientist or physicist or the reading and writing difficulties that can emerge when encountering a discipline for the first time. The same is true in acquiring a trade. Again, with few exceptions, people are trained to be electricians or cosmetologists or nurses but not to teach their occupation.

So it should come as no surprise that even the most committed of new college instructors can be thrown by the variety of needs and limitations some of their students present. As one well-regarded biology teacher told me, when he would find out that a student was having a lot of trouble with the reading, what else could he do but advise that student to drop the class?

Harkening back to my discussion of students in "Who We Are" let me provide an overview of the problems one might find in any given classroom.

First and foremost, some students arrive at college with pretty limited skills, reading at an elementary school level, unable to do more than basic arithmetic, writing undeveloped and error-ridden prose. Students with better literacy and mathematical skills can still have problems with literacy-related academic routines. These can include strategies for reading a textbook, how to use its apparatus (index, glossary), its layout and format, and its illustrations and changes in font to help the reader determine what's more or less important. How to annotate the book and take notes from it also presents challenges for many students. When I was working in tutoring centers, I'd see some students' textbooks that didn't have a mark on the pages, while other students were highlighting three-quarters of nearly every page. Note taking raises similar concerns. Does the student have an effective method: is the notebook page spare, maybe peppered with disconnected bits of information, or is the page an overwhelming blast of script as the student tries feverishly to write down everything the instructor says? Laptops and tablet computers provide some technical enhancements for note takers, but students still have to determine what matters, what's subordinate, what topics go together.

There is also the issue of class requirements and norms, everything from plagiarism, absence, and late policy to assignment due dates and understanding instructions. This all seems pretty straightforward, but it often isn't. Legitimate confusion exists about what constitutes plagiarism, especially for international students or for students with minimal experience writing papers that draw on multiple sources. Students can seriously misjudge the amount of time a new kind of assignment will take. (I see this frequently in occupational classes. A day before an assignment is due in a fashion class, even the most adept students are crazed with half-finished garments.) Something more fundamental and heartbreaking to witness is the frequent mismatch between intellectual strategies that students (including quite successful students) mastered in high school, and the requirements of a seemingly similar—if more advanced—course in college. In the tutorial center at UCLA, we would regularly encounter students from courses like general chemistry who would labor night after night, highlighter in hand, memorizing facts and formulas—and would then fail a test. The test required students to think through a problem and apply what they had learned to solve it. Demonstrating what they had memorized was suddenly not working.

Some students can be reluctant to ask questions, fearful of calling attention to themselves and appearing stupid. These worries can be more acute for those who already feel out of place. We teachers are fond of saying things like "there is no such thing as a stupid question." But let's face it: there are ways to phrase a question that sound smart and mask how little one knows. This is a powerful defensive skill that calls for rhetorical savvy and a sense of academic assurance, the kinds of things that come with a strong education.

A related issue is a reluctance to seek help. This reluctance can be rooted in pride and notions of self-reliance. It can stem from shyness or embarrassment. It can be the result of waning hope. "I sense this heaviness in some of my students," an instructor in a midwestern college tells me. "They are working menial and demeaning jobs and not making enough to survive. They seem overwhelmed and a bit confused." And yet something else can be at play: an unfamiliarity or lack of comfort with help-seeking behavior within institutions. Many students with privileged educational backgrounds are socialized from day one to seek out resources and engage members of institutions to help them attain their goals. This seems so much like second nature to most academics that we forget that it is a culturally influenced, learned behavior.

And finally, there is the complex web of issues involving students' emotional history with school. Is it a history of success and achievement—school as a place where one found safety and affirmation? Or is school a place where, more often than not, one felt awkward, unsure, not all that bright? Insecurity and anxiety can sit behind a whole host of counterproductive behaviors, from not turning in assignments to giving off big-time attitude. And in more than a few cases, the fear and hurt can be crippling.

———

Some of the above requires intervention beyond what the individual instructor can provide—and I'll get to that momentarily.

It is also important to keep in mind the teaching loads full-time community college instructors carry (typically four to five courses per semester) and the fact that the majority of them are part-timers, piecing together a living by teaching at two or more institutions. Still, there are things instructors can do to respond to student need. The suggestions that follow are drawn from the work of people currently in the classroom. They signal a recognition that teaching is more than transmitting a body of knowledge and set of skills but also involves providing entry to the knowledge and skills and tricks of the trade necessary for fuller participation in learning.

Most instructors spend time at the beginning of their classes orienting students to the textbook and other instructional materials or computer-based augmentations, such as class websites and e-portfolios. And given the continual digital divide, careful guidance with online aids is crucial, as is directing students to resources on campus where computers are available.

Some faculty go further and provide instruction on note taking and on reading the textbook (and a few schools offer a one-unit class on reading textbooks in a specific discipline). When I was teaching introductory humanities classes in preparatory programs, I would distribute samples of good notes and not-so-good notes for a particular lesson to make concrete my discussion of note taking. Learning and tutoring centers on many campuses offer workshops on study skills, note taking, and the like, and at some schools, the centers are set up such that the staff can put on a workshop on textbook reading and note taking for particular classes.

It is routine for instructors to go over the syllabus, class requirements, due dates, grading criteria, and so on. Students typically ask a lot of questions, so you've got your audience, providing you with the occasion to dig a little deeper. Explain plagiarism and provide a few examples. Talk about the time it typically takes to complete an assignment. (I saw a fashion instructor take out her daily planner and show her students the way she counts backward from an assignment due date to determine when she needs to begin a project.) And if the expectations for this class, based on your experience, are going to clash with the typical expectations your students bring with them from high school, start addressing the issue now. A speech teacher I met tells her class on the first day that, although they may have been allowed in high school to give a speech by reading it, that won't work now. This is a pretty clear point. But the example I gave earlier about students memorizing chemistry facts and formulas versus solving problems with them will require more careful and illustrated discussion. Let me underscore the *illustrated* part; examples here are key. I've seen math and science instructors demonstrate the difference between memorizing material and using that material in the service of understanding a problem and trying to solve it. It is also necessary to revisit all this—requirements, expectations—once the class is in full swing. The introductory remarks are crucial as orientation, but it all makes much more sense once students have the actual experience of course work.

Instructors routinely list and invite students to come to office hours (which can be a little harder to pull off if you're teaching at three campuses), but some go a few steps further. They explain what office hours are, how they function, and why they're useful. (One instructor explained that some of her students thought you needed to go for the full hour, and if you step back from the term *office hours* for a moment—well, that's a reasonable interpretation if you're unfamiliar with college life.) And some instructors schedule students into appointments, even if it's just a ten- or fifteen-minute consultation—enough to open the pathway. Related to this office hours business, it's not uncommon to establish a formal connection with a writing or tutoring center whereby instructors require students to get tutoring as part of their course work.

Seeking help and asking questions is such dicey territory. Students can be reluctant to speak up or ask for assistance for a wide range of reasons: shyness, fear of revealing ignorance, distaste for claiming the spotlight, cultural norms, codes of masculinity, and more. Students often rely on peers and form their own networks of assistance. That's terrific, and students come to know a lot, everything from how to solve a particular problem to which instructors to avoid. But misinformation can circulate through such networks. And not to enlist faculty help, and especially not to become adept at doing it, is to wall oneself off from valuable intellectual resources—and social resources, as well, for it is often faculty who write letters of recommendation, know about scholarships, internships, and jobs, and can provide introduction to other faculty or student services staff.

Faculty can be hugely instrumental in encouraging and fostering help-seeking behavior. For starters they can discuss this issue directly, providing anecdotes from their own and their past students' experience. If it fits their curriculum, they can even include a reading or writing assignment that addresses the issue. Instructors can ask students to see them and make the appointment on the spot. They can strike up informal conversations before and after class, in the hallway, bumping into a student on campus. A few minutes of conversation where a student feels recognized and acknowledged can have a big effect on someone who has felt like an academic nonperson. "I was so surprised that she knew my name," one student said of his history instructor, "and asked me how the class was going."

Central to these issues is the kind of atmosphere faculty create in their classrooms. This is not simply a question of personal style, persona, or the way one organizes a room—although they all can be factors. I'm talking about the sense students pick up from the way a teacher addresses them, responds to questions, deals with requests. The bottom line for students remains: is this a safe place and do I feel respected? If so, students will be more willing to answer or ask a question, participate, take a chance. And in turn, students pick up on the way a teacher responds to them and tend to replicate it in their interactions with others. I witnessed a striking negative example of this pattern years ago when—to prepare to teach a creative writing class—I sat in on a workshop taught by a well-known local poet. We weren't halfway through the first class, and he had diminished three participants into silence with haughty and snide comments about their work. By the next class, some had dropped, but the telling and disturbing thing is that by the third class those who remained interacted with each other in similarly nasty and unhelpful fashion. The best way to foster civil, thoughtful, intellectually rich discussion is to model it.

There's genuine disagreement among teachers about my next point, but—again, if the atmosphere is right—I'm a big believer in calling on students, particularly those who rarely talk. The idea here is not to put people on the hot seat or indulge in pedagogical *gotcha* but to create a communal conversation and to assist reluctant participants to join in, to speak up. Group work can be useful here, for it provides a smaller, safer space to talk. Of course, there will be initial discomfort, but I've never seen it fail in many years of teaching that the reluctant student eventually begins to volunteer. The classroom is a miniature, temporary society, and I think it is part of our job to help students get comfortable thinking and speaking together in a public space.

To conduct good classroom discussion—especially discussion that includes everyone—the teacher has to listen closely, listen not only to what's said but also to what might be intended but not fully articulated. Then the teacher can assist performance: "Say more, I think I see where you're going." "Don't shut yourself off, you've got a good idea there." "Ah, OK, so let me say it back to you to see if I got it." "I get it, but try this word; does this word help?" Listening closely also enables the teacher to make connections, bringing two students' contributions together, sometimes statements made much earlier or on another day. And students—as would any of us—are impressed and feel validated that a teacher remembered what they said and deemed it worthy enough to put back into play.

All the above seems like a lot, but much of it can be accomplished with some adjustments to that first week or two of class, with a little more focus on getting students to office hours or tutorial centers, and with a greater emphasis on certain kinds of instructional interaction in class. More students coming to office hours will take up more time, but it will pay off in the quality of students' work, which will make the instructor's job more effective and efficient—and more enjoyable. By seeing the role of teacher as an initiator not only to subject matter but to college life, by making the hidden visible, by being systematic in getting students to office hours and tutoring centers, by striking up a casual conversation, by just talking straight about the tricks of the trade, teachers can end up making a big difference in someone's life. Students spend more of their college time with faculty than with any other group on campus. And as my friend Deborah Harrington—who has spent her entire professional life in community colleges—is fond of saying, students succeed one class at a time. Four teachers made my own journey out of high school and through college possible. I truly could not have done it without them.

If faculty can become better teachers by learning about and responding to their students' backgrounds and needs, they can also benefit by thinking in more pedagogically rich ways about their very disciplines.

When I directed the Freshman Composition Program at UCLA, my staff and I organized a gathering where faculty from a wide range of disciplines—English to geography to mathematics—came together to talk about their writing. We asked the participants to bring the early drafts of an article they were currently writing—even if what they had was on bar napkins and the backs of envelopes—and engage with each other in a discussion across disciplines about their process of writing, the way they use it to frame and solve problems, the conventions of argumentation in their discipline, and the difficulties they have with writing. A rich conversation ensued during which people talked about writing from multiple perspectives and heard accounts of writing that in some cases were pretty different from their own. In the afternoon, we asked them to think and talk about the ways their discussion might help them more effectively and creatively use writing in their own courses, from the framing of student assignments to the ways they respond to their students' writing.

This activity enabled faculty members to step outside of their own experiences with writing, to think about writing as *writing*, and to turn what they were coming to understand toward helping their students become better writers—or, at the least, to think more about their students as writers.

A different gathering might ask faculty to reflect on their disciplines, particularly on what it was that first drew them to literature or astronomy or economics. They could be asked to step back and explain as succinctly as they could to those outside their disciplines what the discipline helps us understand about the world, what set of lenses it provides to help us better perceive what surrounds us. Caught up in institutional life, in professional responsibilities, in classes and exams, we can easily lose sight of basic passions and first principles. What is revealed when one looks at the world with an eye to economic trends over time or patterns of social behavior or the workings of biological and physical systems? Participants could then consider ways to revitalize their introductory courses with these basic orientations. For, at the end of the day, the purpose of those courses—especially if they are general education requirements—is not to get students to commit to memory a host of facts about sociology or biology, but to acquire a sociological or biological way of thinking, with all the attendant questions that way of thinking entails.

Of course, you can't teach these disciplinary processes without teaching the "content" of the disciplines themselves. But the above activities can liberate instructors from a slavish commitment to "coverage" and spark useful conversations with their peers about what is essential for students to know in order to understand something about their discipline and how faculty might better invite students into that discipline.

After that workshop on writing, some faculty changed the way they thought about the uses of writing in their courses. After so many years of study, of immersion in a discipline, we can begin to think in pretty narrow ways about writing in academic settings: It's either a specialized pursuit (something we do) or a means by which we evaluate students (something we do to them). What the workshop did was bring back into focus the wide variety of uses of writing—to organize our thoughts, to explore an idea, to express ourselves, to communicate, to record and save—and gave all of us ideas about how to use writing in our classrooms. Some faculty experimented with more creative assignments or built in the opportunity for students to revise what they wrote. And some expanded their uses of writing, working writing into daily classroom activities. After a discussion of a topic, for example, students were given a few minutes to write a brief summary of big concepts or an issue that remained uncovered in the discussion or a question they had. (This technique would work equally well in occupational classes.) Students didn't turn in these small bits of writing but relied on them to guide further discussion or future study, using writing as an aid to thinking and learning.

So much academic professional development is frankly pretty awful—it is short-term, conducted by outsiders, offers a quick fix—and it doesn't speak to basic values that many faculty hold: an investment in their area of expertise and how to teach it better. These values are what brought them into the classroom in the first place, and the most effective faculty development draws on those values. "We don't create spaces on campus where faculty can talk about teaching and learn from each other," a community college vice president told me recently. "We don't cultivate a professional identity around teaching."

_____

Beyond the Individual Course

I am talking with a student in an automotive technology program who, in addition to his occupational certificate, is working toward his associate of science degree. He holds up his right hand, fingers curled in a loose fist, and ticks off the general education courses he's completed. Health, and his index finger straightens out. Music, his second finger. Let's see, oh, history, and his third finger flips up. I ask how he liked the classes, and he says they were OK. I ask about music, and he said he liked getting to play the guitar a little—it was a music appreciation class—for he used to play in church. Health was his first class, so he doesn't remember much about it. History, he's in history now, and there's a paper due next week. He's going to the tutoring center for some help. Tick off the courses. One more out of the way.

Across the wide range of current books critical of higher education, one topic just about all writers agree on is the incoherence and fragmentation of the lower-division curriculum and general education requirements. It is a long-standing complaint; you'll find it in reports on the undergraduate curriculum from the 1950s. There could be many reasons our automotive student didn't particularly take to those general education courses, but his matter-of-fact check-listing of them suggests one considerable problem. They're isolated offerings, each unconnected to the other, bureaucratic requirements with little meaning.

My friend is right; students succeed one class at a time. But students have to take sequences and clusters of courses and do so within time frames and in some cumulative fashion leading toward a certificate or degree. The way those courses fit together, the pathway through them, the information concerning them, and the services surrounding them—all this has a monumental effect on the quality of a student's education. The student I was talking to didn't seem to get a lot out of his health, music, and history classes, but at least he's taking the right courses to meet his goals and doing so in a timely and systematic fashion. Many students take courses out of sequence, or that they didn't need to take, or that have no pattern to them, or that they've taken before. Students do succeed one course at a time, but they can fail when it comes to putting them together in service of a certificate or degree.

So a number of colleges are trying ways to provide at least some coherence to the curriculum, or to crucial segments of the curriculum, like the first semester or year. There is local variation but the general idea is to have students stay together for at least one or two terms as a cohort and to take several courses together, and often the courses have some kind of curricular connection (e.g., a course on American history and a course on American literature) or a subject area course (from political science to nursing) is linked to a writing or mathematics course. Often advising and counseling are also included. Some of these programs (for example, First Year Experience) are open to all students and some are geared toward vulnerable subpopulations such as Puente for Latinos and Umoja for African Americans.

Occupational programs are more coherent by nature, typically having a relatively fixed curriculum (although as students progress there is room for electives) that students take in sequence. But when those students want to get more than an occupational certificate, they face the same array of general education courses and the same problems of coherence and fragmentation. There is a move to link some writing and mathematics courses and even some traditional general education courses to the occupations; for example, health or humanities courses to automotive or construction trades. And, as I discussed in a previous chapter, there is a lot of effort these days to link writing and mathematics courses to occupational courses, to "contextualize" writing and mathematics in the work of the electrician, the chef, the nurse.

These linkages can lack substance, but they can also be intellectually vital. If faculty from across subject areas are able to think through and plan the linkage—and be compensated for it—they can develop classroom activities that authentically represent the intellectual demands of the workplace and, conversely, bring academic content to life through occupational tasks and simulations. Imagine how the house or the automobile or the computer could be the core of a rich, integrated curriculum: one that includes social and technical history, science and economics, and hands-on assembly and repair. Instructors would learn about new subjects and make unfamiliar connections: the historian investigates the health care or travel industry, or the machinist engages the humanities. Basic mathematical skill would be fostered along with an appreciation of mathematics, a mathematical sensibility, through the particulars of the automotive garage, the restaurant, the hospital lab.

A lot of experimentation is going on with basic-skills instruction. Some of us have been critical of traditional curriculum and instruction in remedial mathematics, reading, and English for a long time, but now national attention is being paid to the issue. So some institutions have set up a system whereby high school students can concurrently enroll in college basic-skills courses to get a jump on remediation. Other campuses allow students who test low to enroll in the regular freshman course in math or English and provide additional instructional and tutorial support. And others are attempting to connect the skills courses to content courses or to combine or reconceive and intensify courses so that students take fewer of them, a process frequently referred to as "acceleration."

As with any reform, these models can be enacted superficially or with care and depth. The fear about shortening the sequences of remedial courses is that students will be rushed through a curriculum when some of those students have pretty severe needs.

"Acceleration" is in hindsight probably a poor choice of a label for this process, for it can imply a mindless tromping down of the throttle. And, in fact, in some schools the need for resources drives administrators to shorten sequences without giving much thought to the content of the newly accelerated courses. The goal of any of these new approaches should not only be efficiency but, as well, a rethinking of the curriculum itself. We will not have made much progress if students concurrently enroll or receive additional support or take intensified classes in a shortened sequence, *but the remedial curriculum remains the same.* The best accelerated programs involve both a rethinking of sequences and a rethinking of the curriculum of the courses within the sequence.

This discussion of sequences of courses and structured programs intersects with another, broader debate going on right now about the amount of structure versus choice students should have in selecting their course of study, for the standard model of the wide-ranging curriculum from which students can choose, explore, and experiment can have a powerful downside. Perhaps college, or some colleges and programs, should be much more constrained and directed.

The sociologist James Rosenbaum and his colleagues point out that successful private occupational colleges tend to have a more structured curriculum, more directive advising, and more lock-step pathways—and some of these institutions have a higher rate of completion. Rosenbaum's work is provocative because certain for-profit colleges have been charged with unethical practices and also because the kind of structure he advocates flies in the face of a venerable element of the college ethos: the freedom for students to try things out, discover new interests. But Rosenbaum is absolutely right that the records of many of the students who don't make it reveal an unproductive patchwork of courses. By and large these students have limited knowledge about how college works as well as limited time and resources to invest in postsecondary education.

The fundamental issue—and it is a thorny one—is the tension between choice and structure, which becomes all the more complicated when we're talking about populations who not infrequently have been treated by the state and by educational institutions in ways that constrain their agency, their freedoms and choices. Curriculum tracking in high school is one example. So some of us worry when we see a matriculation scheme that pretty much removes the choice and decision making from a student's pathway through college. Yet decisions about courses and services are best made when people have good information and have basic needs secured. Some of the students I've been concerned with in this book have neither, with resulting erratic and unproductive course selection and a graveyard's worth of unachieved goals. So Rosenbaum and company have a compelling argument when they suggest that college should compensate for students' lack of knowledge about higher education and their resulting counterproductive decisions by structuring the college experience for them.

As with so many debates in education, the answer involves a fusion of the two poles of the argument. Even the most job-oriented people can discover things about themselves, find new interests, change occupational goals, decide for the first time in their lives that they want to pursue further education. We want to be careful not to diminish the possibility of those discoveries by overstructuring the college experience. Furthermore, how will students develop some degree of savvy navigating institutions if the environment is so constrained that they have little need to learn how to do it?

Clearly, the situation we have now on many campuses is too unstructured; there are too many possibilities for students to get lost in courses, administrative routines, institutional folkways. One of the benefits of the kinds of programs I've been discussing—those that place students in cohorts, that link some courses, that teach math and English in a meaningful context, that have advising and counseling wrapped in—is that such programs provide both structure and some room to move, opportunities to learn how to survive in institutions but with supports and advocates when a student falters. The problem is that such programs are costly and may serve as little as 10 percent of an institution's student body. So as we continue to explore ways to keep students in school and help them succeed, we move to the level of the institution, to deans and provosts and presidents.

Institutional Vision

About thirty years ago, John Chaffee, a young philosophy instructor at LaGuardia Community College in Queens, New York, began teaching a traditional introductory course in philosophy only to realize that many of his students didn't have the academic preparation to handle the curriculum. It was a grueling experience for him and, one imagines, for his students as well. But Chaffee believed that "philosophy is for everybody," so he took several steps back and began to develop a course in critical thinking to build the reading, writing, and analytical skills necessary to handle further philosophy courses and other humanities and social science courses as well. He was determined to make philosophy relevant to the lives of his working-class students, many of whom were the first in their families to go to college. Over the years, he refined the course, wrote a textbook for it, pursued outside grants, got involved in and helped shape a national critical thinking movement, became department chair, hired more faculty, developed or revived other courses in philosophy (ethics, aesthetics, law, logic), and began to plan for courses in Eastern, African, and Latin American philosophy—which are now in place. The presidents he's worked for recognized the merits of his efforts, provided further support, and saw philosophy as an integral part of the educational mission of the college. Now 150 sections of philosophy and critical thinking courses are offered a year, enrolling 4,500 students. LaGuardia has sixty students majoring in philosophy, a philosophy club, a student journal, and a yearly conference. Most colleges and universities don't come close to generating that level of interest in philosophy.

The story of philosophy at LaGuardia represents a number of the themes and qualities that, to my mind, lie at the core of effective leadership at the people's college, beginning with a belief in the ability of the college's students. Too often we make judgments about students such as those at LaGuardia that limit their development: first generation, working-class students are focused on preparation for practical careers, or most haven't had the kind of K–12 education that would develop in them an appreciation for subjects like philosophy. There's some truth to these claims, but they become dangerous when they close down rather than open up thinking about students and the possibilities of their curriculum. Some faculty and counselors worry about students getting in over their heads, needing to avoid difficult courses, making it through the system—possibly a well-intentioned but ultimately profoundly restricting set of beliefs. And, finally, some faculty just hold flat-out ugly attitudes toward the students in their charge. Chaffee tells me about attending a conference where he heard a philosophy professor quip that his students weren't fit to sweep out the Augean stables, a reference to Hercules' fifth labor, clearing away huge amounts of animal dung. (Ironically, Hercules accomplishes the task with great ingenuity—he reroutes two rivers through the stables—suggesting that the professor misjudges his students' intelligence after all, and that he might need to brush up on his Greek mythology.) What the people at LaGuardia did was provide a stunning refutation of all these beliefs and a powerful affirmation of what our students can achieve.

In this example, we also see creativity in thinking about one's discipline and its potential meaning for one's students. Philosophy so easily and so often becomes a rarified pursuit, suited for specialists only. But, the LaGuardia people thought, what is more relevant to the lives of its Queens students than these questions: "Who am I?" "How can I find my life's work?" "What is my moral compass?" "What is true?"

The brochure that details LaGuardia's philosophy curriculum prominently offers a pragmatic rationale: that philosophy prepares one for further academic study, is "the ultimate work skill," and, according to the *Times* of London, increases one's "employ-ability rate." Such a pitch is not at all surprising given the increased economic justification in the United States for all levels of schooling, K–16. But that same brochure offers other justifications as well, ones involving intellectual, social, and moral development. "Find your path, philosophically." "How can I create a meaningful life?" Students in the major automatically become members of a monthly seminar called Community of Thinkers. Right along with career advancement comes the opportunity to reflect on the notion of career itself and the relation of the work we do to who we are and who we want to become. The people's college, of course, exists to assist students in becoming more economically viable. But its mission must be broader than economic development alone.

Many discussions of leadership focus at the top, the level of the president or chancellor. The vision from the top is important, to be sure, but I've become increasingly interested in middle management and below: the dean, the department chair, the individual faculty member. I've recently attended several statewide gatherings of faculty and staff from California's sprawling system of community colleges (California holds about one-tenth of the nation's two-year colleges), and I've been knocked out by the faith in student ability, the on-the-ground wisdom, the visionary energy of the faculty and counselors, the tutorial center and special-projects directors I've met there. People attending such conferences, of course, are a select group, but collectively they remind one of the extraordinary educational creativity that resides in this dynamic segment of an institution. The philosophy project at LaGuardia began with one new instructor. Fortunately, the college's presidents noticed and encouraged his idea. A sign of a vibrant institution is an openness at the top to ideas emerging from those closest to the students themselves.

This frontline to mid-level domain is also roiling with protection of turf, with entrenched political conflict, with interpersonal rivalries and animosities. I think it was the American philosopher George Santayana who observed that academic politics are so nasty because the stakes are so small. In addition to local politics, traditions and ossified routines also form barriers to the realization of good ideas. I've heard so many stories of department chairs or deans quashing innovative curricula, cooperation between departments, or fresh ways to deliver services. Some of the people at those California conferences were calling for strong professional development at this mid-level of administration to address these problems and to focus on how to recognize and foster talent. But moderating turf conflict and rivalry also requires strong leadership from the top.

From consideration of the physical layout of the campus to the creation of interdepartmental programs, community colleges need a way of seeing that begins with the student and is directed toward the student's fullest possible development. I think here of a young woman who, after a pleasant but fairly empty exchange with someone in her college's transfer center, wondered "if that person really cared about what happens to me." This chapter has been a partial catalogue of ways that staff and faculty in various niches at various institutional levels can respond affirmatively to that student's desire.

To bring these levels together, to orient an entire campus toward understanding student need and fostering student development requires high-level leadership and, because so many departments and individual players are involved, takes a long, politically savvy, carefully executed process of planning. Difficult as this is, it is not impossible.

One example is Valencia College in Orlando, Florida. A lot has been written about Valencia, but, for our purposes, I'll touch on two things. In line with the earlier discussion about finding a balance between the smorgasbord curriculum of the traditional college and the tightly structured pathway of some for-profit colleges, Valencia has developed a matriculation process whereby students make their choices within more defined curricular pathways—pathways aimed at specific beneficial goals. For example, if you want to get an occupational certificate, you are also guided toward the general education courses required to get an associate's degree—and these courses transfer to all state colleges in Florida so that further study remains open. Students have choices, but they are strategically bounded and directed by the institution. Also, because the college staff saw that students historically were having a hard time with mathematics, with many never making it out of the remedial sequence of basic courses—they put considerable effort into getting students up to par early. Mathematics is a skill crucial to many occupations and academic majors—and transfer-level math is a core requirement for most four-year colleges—so hitting this gateway requirement early and hard is another way to keep students on track.

The second thing to mention, and to me the more remarkable, is the degree of coordination among campus units in the service of helping students meet their goals. From signs on the campus, to professional development for faculty, to the thoughtful use of on-line advising and planning aids, the pieces work together in service of fostering student progress. All of this represents a monumental institutional undertaking spanning about ten years, and Valencia did receive considerable philanthropic support along the way, but the changes would not have occurred without a vision of what could be possible, a vision combining idealism with political skill and organizational wisdom.

When a colleague of mine visited Valencia a short while ago, she found herself at the end of the day, after crossing and criss-crossing the campus, thinking, "My God, these students are go-ing to make it." The overall poor success rates of our community colleges have sparked a host of reform efforts across the country. Some come from community college personnel and some high-profile ones are coming from state legislators. The government initiatives vary, but they tend to target admissions policy or place restrictions on courses students can take or set performance goals and tie some budgetary incentive to them. The proposals have some worthwhile ideas within them, and let us grant that all of them are well intentioned. But, as we have been witnessing for a decade in K–12 schools under No Child Left Behind, broadscale mandates enacted without deep knowledge of on-the-ground con-ditions and practices can have harmful, unintended consequences.

Standardized tests of basic skills, for example, in some schools have resulted in a narrowing of the curriculum. As I have noted elsewhere in this book, proposals to put a limit on who the colleges accept will result in the most needy people being left without instruction. A blanket concentration on increasing transfer rates will drain resources and effort away from occupational programs. Tying resources to completion rates will lead institutions to accept only those students who are better prepared. The solutions to the problems of the community college will require fewer blunt policy instruments and more creative solutions formed in concert with the exceptional work already being done by those in classrooms, tutoring centers, and counseling offices.

The further problem is that the reform initiatives from on high, as I've noted, reflect a strictly economic view of education. I have been privy to numerous policy discussions over the past few years and have yet to hear much of anything that addresses the humanity of the people in the classroom. My concern is not just a stylistic one; the way we talk about education affects what we do and the way we do it. It would be valuable to hear occasionally the kind of talk, and thus vision, that could guide a newly hired philosophy instructor to wonder how he could create the conditions for a broad range of students rigorously to explore how to lead a meaningful life—and that, in turn, would lead a college president to say, *Yes, this is who we are.*

A Learning Society

The farmer, the mechanic, the manufacturer, the merchant, the sailor, the soldier . . . must be educated.

—*Philip Lindsley, president of the University of Nashville, 1825*

SINCE THE EARLY DAYS of the Republic, adult Americans have been seeking ways to further educate themselves after their (successful or unsuccessful) formal education is over. The motives vary and combine—intellectual stimulation, social benefit, or occupational advancement through the learning of specific job skills—but the bottom line is that we as a people seem driven toward self-improvement and have created a staggering number of ways, both superficial and substantial, to achieve it: from self-help books to correspondence courses to continuous incarnations of mutual-improvement societies (lyceums, mechanics' institutes, chautau-quas) to classes in university extension.

Unions such as the Knights of Labor and farmers' political organizations, most notably the Grange, had considerable educational programs. There was the public-library movement and agricultural extensions and experimental colleges for working people.

Private occupational or proprietary schools arose and grew. The public community college began in 1901 and expanded rapidly through the mid-twentieth century, and the GI bill opened two- and four-year colleges to a remarkable number of returning veterans, changing the nature of American higher education in the process. There are literacy programs and workforce development initiatives and adult schools that offer everything from basic education to courses on local geography, French cooking, and navigating the Internet. As historian Joseph Kett put it in *The Pursuit of Knowledge Under Difficulties*, a sweeping account of this multistrand tradition, in the same way that "democracy seems only to whet appetites for more democracy," so too "each advance in educational opportunity" sparks a desire for more education. The people we've met in this book are the newest participants in this tradition.

As we've seen, many of the reasons this new generation needs to pursue a second chance are deeply troubling: inadequate K–12 schools, limited youth programs, unemployment, and the effects of poverty on neighborhoods and families. Furthermore, the sheer numbers of people involved strain an already overloaded system; yet the system has to respond, because there is a lot riding on their success, for them and for our economic and social structure. Especially in these recessionary times, the influx of all these students—many in need of academic remediation and other services—is a source of great consternation to policy makers and educational administrators. Just about everything I've read or heard on the topic frames it as a problem.

While acknowledging the significant budgetary and institutional challenges involved, it is also possible, shifting to the historical perspective provided by Joseph Kett, to view the swelling enrollments in a positive light. This new population is more diverse—especially by race and ethnicity—than most of those who have participated in nontraditional American educational movements and institutions in the past. People like those in this book represent an advance in educational opportunity, an example of educational democracy whetting the appetite for more access, more possibility, more of a chance to learn new skills, master new bodies of knowledge. As one of the students we met earlier put it, she wants to be able to take tests and write essays "like it is part of my life."

To realize the promise of a second-chance education for this new population, we will need to do a number of things. The first few of these won't cost much at all, but might be among the most difficult to realize, for they call for a shift in ways of thinking. The good news is that multiple examples of these shifts in thinking are already occurring in classrooms and programs around the United States, exemplars that we can learn from, that can open up our educational imagination.

———

Let us begin with first principles. While acknowledging the importance of the economic motive for schooling, our philosophy of education—our guiding rationale for creating schools—has to include the intellectual, social, civic, moral, and aesthetic motives as well. If these further motives are not articulated, they fade from public policy, from institutional mission, from curriculum development. Without this richer philosophy, those seeking a second chance will likely receive a bare-bones, strictly functional education, one that does not honor the many reasons they return to school and, for that matter, one not suitable for a democratic society.

We'll also need to fundamentally rethink the divide between the academic and vocational courses of study, an arbitrary but quite consequential way of separating kinds of knowledge. This rethinking will of necessity involve scrutiny of the long-standing Western separation of physical from mental activity and the beliefs about intelligence and the social order that accompany that separation.

We need to take basic-skills instruction out of the hinterland of higher education, liberate it from the academic snobbery and bankrupt assumptions about teaching and learning that profoundly limit its effectiveness. To do this does not signal complacency about the conditions that lead to academic underpreparation but acknowledges the fact that we've never had a period in our history when remediation has been unnecessary—so we had better get good at it if we want to maintain educational opportunity. This is not just a subject matter or institutional issue, but a civic and moral issue as well.

Two other efforts are necessary to realize this recasting of basic-skills instruction, and these will cost money. First, the need for substantial professional development is overwhelming. I've seen so many committed, hard-working teachers using reductive skills and drills curricula because that's what was given to them, and that's all they know. Because basic-skills instruction is held in such low regard, and its cookbook, scripted curriculum is so transportable, it's assumed that anyone can teach it. The second point concerns the use of computer technology in basic-skills instruction. The technology holds great promise, but we must keep in mind that any technology is only as good as the thinking behind it and the use made of it. If computer technology, as sophisticated as it can be, is used in ways that simply reflect the same old reductive beliefs about cognition and remediation, then it won't move us forward at all. Changing both beliefs and practices in remedial education and creating good technology and meaningfully integrating it into curriculum will require human and fiscal resources.

To think clearly about the debate over college for all versus occupational training—and thus to come to a fruitful path beyond the debate—we'll need to be mindful of several things. Part of the problem is that our society does not provide a range of options after high school for young people to grow in productive ways, to learn about the world and about their talents and interests. We lack, for example, a robust system of occupational apprenticeships or a comprehensive national service program. The deep-rooted divide between the academic and vocational courses of study—and the social-class biases reflected in that divide—also complicate the debate. We won't be able to create more imaginative postsecondary options for young people until we address this divide. Another issue to consider is this: It took a long time and a good deal of effort to initiate a cultural shift so that a wider sweep of our population began to see college as a possibility. We need to be alert to the unintended consequences of altering that cultural shift. Finally, we have to be aware of the fact that this debate is not simply an economic one but one that is taking place against a backdrop of discrimination. The debate about who should be educated and to what end has powerful legal, social, and civic dimensions to it.

The relationship between poverty and academic achievement is a long-standing issue in K–12 education, and, unfortunately, in some recent school-reform debates the relationship has devolved into an unproductive binary. One position claims that poverty so devastates students' lives that achievement is virtually impossible. The other holds that if schools are run well, poverty is not a barrier to learning. Variations of this simplistic rendering play out in discussions of adult and postsecondary education as well—and the results are just as counterproductive.

Poverty does provide a rationale for some instructors and administrators to avoid challenging curricula and programs, to not push either themselves or their students toward excellence, to perpetuate an institutional culture of resignation. Conversely, a simplified view of poverty and achievement—a radically individualist model of mobility—flies in the face of common sense. Zip code might not be destiny, but it does correlate with stability of housing and employment, with health care, with environmental threats, with three square meals a day—all of which affect the time students have to attend classes, study, get assistance, concentrate, even just see clearly the print on the pages of their textbooks. To realize the promise of a second-chance education, we'll need to create the best programs we can and provide adequate financial aid, support services, and a social safety net to enable people to attend and thrive in them.

There can be a conflict between access—removing barriers to participation in school—and standards. There is no easy resolution to this conflict, but what we can do is keep both goals equally in sight, committing to both admitting people and educating them well. And when a standard is put in place that has the potential to enhance the quality of education for some—for example, increasing the literacy and mathematics content of the GED examination—we also have to create opportunities for those whose knowledge is not yet at the level of the new exam.

Institutions that serve a primarily second-chance population have to orient themselves as best they can on all levels—from physical layout, to guidance and counseling, to curriculum design, to professional development—to the populations they serve. Many such institutions claim to do this already, and some do so masterfully. But, in line with my observations about poverty and achievement, this orientation needs to be one that both meets people where they are *and* moves them forward to fulfilling their goals—and possibly opens up new goals for them.

There is much talk in our time of the United States becoming a "learning society." Management consultants write about "organizational learning," and adult development experts champion "lifelong learning." The focus of this talk tends to be on professionals and managers and people with a baccalaureate degree and beyond—mostly members of the middle and upper-middle classes. But if we're serious about our country being a learning society, then we need to include all of its members, "the farmer, the mechanic, the manufacturer. . . ."

───────────

It rained last night, but this morning the sun is out, reflecting off water pooled in endless little pits and recesses across the campus. A man with a bulky sweatshirt bearing the college's logo is walking with his daughter, his hand between her shoulders, toward the elementary school a few blocks away. He's telling her he'll pick her up once his classes are over, and then they start laughing about something I can't hear. Further into the campus, right by the three-story Construction Trades Building, a group of four men and a woman are walking toward the stairwell, toolbelts around their waists or slung over their shoulders. Two guys on the top-floor walkway yell down to them. At the Automotive Trades Building next door, an older man is bending down to look at the undercarriage of a city bus up on lifts.

Turn east toward the library, which isn't open yet, and you see six or so students sitting on stone benches bent over textbooks. A guy on a cell phone has his right foot back against the wall, a cigarette in his free hand: "Cuz I messed up, that's why." Two women walk by, "We both gotta do it," one says emphatically to the other. "One can't be thinkin' one way, and one thinkin' the other." Over at the Fashion Building, several women sit on the stairs, their transparent plastic toolboxes in their laps. And close to the Humanities Building a row of student nurses are lined up at the coffee cart.

I see Sam, one of the students I know from the welding program, the fellow we met earlier in Chapter Six who had such a difficult time trying to see a counselor. He is talking to two older women. He sees me and calls me over. He has been taking additional courses to get his associate of science degree, and he's done so well that, with the recommendation of his welding instructor, he got a job tutoring in the reading center. That's where he met these women, Dorothy and Zoe—and they are something, rambunctious, funny, lots to say. . . especially about Sam, whom they praise as a great tutor. Sam begins to help Dorothy figure out what classes to take next term, so I talk briefly to Zoe—blue nail polish, cigarette—about the basic-skills courses she has to take. She gets serious and says she wants to learn math, finally wants to learn it. She likes coming to the college, she continues, "didn't know it would be this good." She waves her hand across the area with the coffee cart, the library benches, the stairs to the Humanities Building. "I like it. This is nice."

Sam and I excuse ourselves and walk into Humanities where his English class will start in a few minutes. He tells me that the work in the reading center has blown him away. What an "honor" it is to help people—especially people older than him—develop a skill that they'll use the rest of their lives. The tutoring has made him want to become a better writer, too. He sees how important writing can be. He's been talking to both his welding instructor and the head of the reading center about getting a bachelor's degree in counseling or adult education or something that will enable him to continue to do this work, helping other people become better educated. Maybe he can support himself as a welder while he's in school. "Who knows," he says. "I never thought I'd be doing this."

A phrase you'll read in educational tracts from right after the Revolutionary War and into the 1820s and 1830s is "the general diffusion of knowledge," a call to spread learning across the young Republic. Though expressed in sweeping terms, this democratizing of knowledge didn't apply to all, either by law or because of the realities of social stratification. Sam and Dorothy and Zoe are pursuing their goals within the constraints of the social order as well, but opportunities are open to them that weren't there for their forebears, and they are embracing these opportunities. Will the college provide them with the kinds of instruction and services they need? Will they be able to keep food on the table and a roof over their head? Will there be decent work for them at the end of their journey? We live up to our egalitarian ideals when the answer is yes.

The students on this campus carry more than their fair share of hardship and sorrow, and the odds of success are stacked against them. But hope and a sense of the future are here in equal measure. Will we give these students a vital second chance—and through them realize the second time around a broadscale societal commitment to the general diffusion of knowledge?

ACKNOWLEDGMENTS

First things first. Without the good people at The New Press, *Back to School* wouldn't exist. Here's to the publisher, Ellen Adler, for supporting this book from the beginning, and to editor Tara Grove for words of encouragement all along the way. Maury Botton, Cinqué Hicks, and Bob Anderson masterfully took the book through production.

I owe more than I can say to Diane Wachtell, my editor now for two books, for her belief in my work and, once again, for being so astute, from overall structure to the level of the sentence. Thank you, Diane. Thank God you're in publishing.

I use pseudonyms for all the students in *Back to School*, so I can't acknowledge them by name, but without their generosity and openness, there would be no story to tell. I only hope I have done right by them.

Many, many teachers, counselors, and administrators contributed to the book by inviting me into their institutions and classrooms. I am deeply grateful to: Leticia Barajas, Juan Bautista, Chrissie Blount, Steve Blount, Mary Brand, Cecilia Carbajal, Roland Chapdelaine, Akiko Cybulski, Christie Dam,

Tessie Fernando, Jan Gangel-Vasquez, Ron Jackson, Kimberly James, Paula Johnson, Armando Mendez, Shelley Mitzman, Lisa Moreno, Dorothy Smith, Ron Stringer, and Ruth Watanabe.

I want to pay special tribute to those whose classrooms and offices were open to me for long stretches of time, enabling me to witness a story unfold: Jah' Shams Abdul-Mumin, Carole Anderson, Che Chancy, Finna Drebskaya, Maryanne Galindo, Jess Guerra, Tiffany Jackson, Lisa Legohn, Roberto Mancia, Nicki McBreen, Danny Moynahan, Dave Robinson, Leila Rosemberg, Delia Thornton, Allison Tom-Miura, Carolyn Washington, and Rita Weingourt. I benefited immensely from their deep knowledge, which they freely shared.

Finally, let me thank Marcy Drummond and Deborah Harrington, who know more than I can ever hope to about the community college, and who, though busy beyond belief, gave generously of their time.

I enjoyed and learned from long conversations with Linda Adler-Kassner, Rose Asara, Shannon Allen, Kathy Booth, David Charlson, Luis Chavez, Tina Christie, Linda Collins, John Conner, Becky Cox, Regina Deil-Amen, Patricia Gandara, Karen Givven, Joanna Goode, Val Harris, Katie Hern, Michael Katz, Jane Margolis, Pat McDonough, Leslee Oppenheim, Gary Orfield, Cathy Pack, Julie Phelps, Michelle Pilati, Cynthia Ramirez, Laura Reinhardt, Jan Resseger, Gwendelyn Rivera, Nancy Shulock, Peter Simon, Cheryl Smith, Wendy Smith, Myra Snell, Jim Stigler, Deborah Stipek, Belinda Thompson, Michael Walzer, and Jeff Wood. Thanks to Rebecca Mlynarczyk for lending a hand with the *Journal of Basic Writing*. And a big heap of gratitude to

Julian Betts, Jennie Brand, Michael Seltzer, and especially Jordan Rickles for help with analyzing the research on the economic benefits of the GED exam.

I was also fortunate to have a number of very wise people read earlier drafts of some of the chapters: Peter Dow Adams, Manuel Espinoza, Ed Frankel, Jan Frodesen, John Garvey, Sara Goldrick-Rab, Kris Gutierrez, Casandra Harper, Jack McFarland, Pam Schuetz, Anne Vo, and Shirin Vossoughi. They made the writing stronger.

Some of the research involved in *Back to School* has been supported over the years by The Spencer Foundation. That foundation has made much of my work possible. Over the last two years, I have been fortunate to be part of the UC ACCORD Pathways to Postsecondary Success Project, funded by the Bill and Melinda Gates Foundation. Hilary Pennington and Ann Person were directly involved in the project, much to the project's benefit. If we're lucky, every once in a while we fall in with a great group of co-workers, and that was the case here. Many thanks to the principal investigators on the project, Amanda Datnow and Danny Solorzano, and to my wonderful teammates: Lluliana Alonso, Christine Cerven, Maritza del Razo, Nicki Johnson-Ahorlu, Makeba Jones, Maria Malagon, Bud Mehan, Jen Nations, Kelly Nielson, Lindsay Perez Huber, Yen Ling Shek, Veronica Velez, and Susan Yonozawa. A special tip of the hat to the two project directors, Vicki Park and Tara Watford. My notebooks are full of their wisdom.

An earlier version of Chapter Three, "Full Cognitive Throttle," appeared in the *American Scholar* as "Making Sparks Fly," and an earlier version of Chapter Five "Overcoming Bad Ideas," appeared in *Mind, Culture, and Activity*. Chapter Two, "Who Should Go to College?" is drawn from commentaries that first appeared in *Teachers College Record* and *Education Week*. I am grateful for these earlier publications and for the assistance their editors gave me.

I had the benefit of terrific research assistance, helping me run down statistics and information on particular regions and institutions. Thank you, Matt Stevens, Tiffany Cheng, Ashley Luu, and, right at the end with rockets blasting, Denise Pacheco, who also kept me sane while compiling endnotes. And a special thank you to Liz Alvarado for generously sharing her observations on one of the schools.

Through the two years of writing, Kim Mattheussens has been a great help when I was on the road, enabling me keep all the balls in the air. Ditto for Christina Bebensee, who came on like gangbusters during the last six months and did a first-class job preparing the final draft of the manuscript.

Introduction

7   "Recently, a flurry of books . . .": See, for example, Andrew Hacker and Claudia Dreifus, *Higher Education? How Colleges Are Wasting Our Money and Failing Our Kids—and What We Can Do About It* (New York: Times Books, 2011); Mark C. Taylor, *Crisis on Campus: A Bold Plan for Reforming Our Colleges and Universities* (New York: Knopf, 2010); Richard Arum and Josipa Roksa, *Academically Adrift: Limited Learning on College Campuses* (Chicago: University of Chicago Press, 2011).

8   "Here are two telling statistics . . .": Sara Goldrick-Rab and Kia Sorensen, "Unmarried Parents in College," *Future of Children*, vol. 20, no. 2, 2010, 179–203; and Ronald A. Phipps, "Remedial Education in Colleges and Universities: What's Really Going On?" *The Review of Higher Education*, vol. 24, no. 1, Fall 2000, 67–85.

9   "But the majority of the more than 10 million students . . .": "The Condition of Education, Special Analysis" (Washington, DC: U.S. Department of Education, National Postsecondary Student Aid Study, 2002), Table 2: Percentage of all undergraduates with each nontraditional characteristic, by type of institution, and percentage

of nontraditional undergraduates with each nontraditional characteristic, by nontraditional characteristic and status: 1999–2000.

9   "As a steady stream of reports on the American economy. . .": See, for example, Colleen Moore, Jeremy Offenstein, and Nancy Shulock, "Consequence of Neglect: Performance Trends in California Higher Education" (Sacramento, CA: Institute for Higher Education Leadership and Policy, July 2011).

10   "Community college graduation rates . . . about 30 percent . . .": Laura G. Knapp, Janice E. Kelly-Reid, and Scott A. Ginder, "Enrollment in Postsecondary Institutions, Fall 2009; Graduation Rates, 2003 and 2006 Cohorts; and Financial Statistics, Fiscal Year 2009" (Washington, DC: U.S. Department of Education, National Center for Education Statistics, February 2011).

14   ". . .60 percent of community college students attend more than one community college. . .": Clifford Adelman, *Moving into Town—and Moving On: The Community College in the Lives of Traditional-Age Students* (Washington, DC: U.S. Department of Education, 2005), xv.

14   ". . .efforts to develop more discrete indicators . . .": Colleen Moore, Nancy Shulock, and Jeremy Offenstein, "Steps to Success: Analyzing Milestone Achievement to Improve Community College Student Outcomes" (Sacramento, CA: Institute for Higher Education Leadership and Policy, October 2009).

16   "The headlines on . . .": Carla Rivera, "Billions Spent in the U.S. on Community College Students Who Drop Out," *Los Angeles Times*, October 20, 2011; Joanna Jacobs,

"Failing Students Get Federal Aid," *Community College Spotlight,* April 28, 2011.

17 "In *Ragged Dick* . . .": Richard Fink, ed., *Ragged Dick and Mark, the Match Boy: Two Novels by Horatio Alger* (New York: Collier Books, 1962), 108.

17 "How noteworthy it is then . . .": Scott Winship, "Mobility Impaired: The American Dream Must Move from the Bottom Up," *National Review,* November 14, 2011, 30–33.

18 "The *Economist,* not as fiscally. . .": "What's Wrong with the American Economy?" *Economist,* April 30–May 6, 2011, 11–12, 75–77.

19 "One more thing.": American Library Association, "A Perfect Storm Brewing: Budget Cuts Threaten Public Library Services at Time of Increased Demand" (Chicago: Funding and Technology Access Study, 2009–2010).

20 ". . . Los Angeles Unified School District is considering eliminating . . .": City News Service, "LAUSD to Consider Parcel Tax Measure," *EGPNews,* February 16, 2012, http://egpnews.com/2012/02/lausd-to-consider-parcel-tax-measure/.

20 ". . . as Rep. Paul Ryan puts it . . .": Michael Tomasky, "GOP Set to Self-Destruct," *Daily Beast,* November 29, 2011.

21 "Recent studies . . . parental income . . .": "Ever Higher Society, Ever Harder to Ascend," *Economist,* January 1, 2005.

21 "A report from the Pell Institute . . .": "Developing 20/20 Vision on the 2020 Degree Attainment Goal," (Washington, DC: Pell Institute, May 2011).

22 Richard J. Hernstein and Charles Murray, *The Bell Curve: Intelligence and Class Structure in American Life* (New York: Free Press, 1994).

24 "Not many boys can expect . . .": Fink, *Ragged Dick and Mark, the Match Boy*, 30.

27 "A particularly trenchant critique . . .": Gordon Lafer, *The Job Training Charade* (Ithaca, NY: Cornell University Press, 2002).

29 "One study suggests . . .": Adelman, *Moving into Town*, xvi.

Chapter I

35 ". . . a little over four thousand adult education programs . . .": Lennox McLendon, "Adult Student Waiting List Survey" (Washington, DC: National Council of State Directors of Adult Education, 2009–2010).

43 "By one estimate, only 10 percent . . .": Robert Balfanz et al., "Grad Nation: A Guidebook to Help Communities Tackle the Dropout Crisis" (Washington, DC: America's Promise Alliance, February 2009).

44 "(about 7 percent of the population held a degree)": Joseph Kett, *The Pursuit of Knowledge Under Difficulties: From Self-Improvement to Adult Education in America, 1750–1990* (Stanford, CA: Stanford University Press, 1994), 250.

44 "Approximately 40 million American . . .": Catherine Gewertz, "Higher Education Is Goal of GED Overhaul," *Education Week*, November 16, 2011.

44 "People, who, . . . gain the most labor market benefit . . .": Richard J. Murnane, John B. Willett, and John H. Taylor, "Who Benefits from Obtaining a GED? Evidence from High School and Beyond," *Review of Economics and Statistics*, vol. 82, no. 1, 2000.

45 "The goal of the reformers . . .": Gewertz, "Higher Education Is Goal of GED Overhaul."

46   "... 160,000 people on waiting lists ...": McLendon, "Adult Student Waiting List Survey."

47   "... James Heckman argues ...": James J. Heckman, John Eric Humphries, and Nicholas S. Mader, "The GED," National Bureau of Economic Research, Working Paper 16064, June 2010.

47   "... McGraw-Hill Research Foundation ...": Lennox McLendon, Debra Jones, and Mitch Rosin, "The Return on Investment (ROI) from Adult Education and Training: Measuring the Economic Impact of a Better Education and Trained U.S. Workforce," policy paper, McGraw Hill Research Foundation, no date.

51   "Historian Harvey Graff ...": Harvey Graff, *The Literacy Myth: Literacy and Social Structure in the Nineteenth Century* (New York: Academic Press, 1979).

Chapter 2

58   "The skeptics are a diverse . . .": See, for example, Richard Vedder, "Overinvesting in Higher Ed," *Forbes*, August 30, 2010.

59   "... a book of mine ...": Mike Rose, *The Mind at Work: Valuing the Intelligence of the American Worker* (New York: Viking, 2004).

61   "As the authors of . . .": *Vocational-Technical Education: Major Reforms and Debates, 1917–Present* (Reports prepared for the Office of Vocational and Adult Education, U.S. Department of Education, 1993), 7.

62   "Research by sociologists ...": Jennie E. Brand and Yu Xie, "Who Benefits Most from College? Evidence for Negative Selection in Heterogeneous Economic Returns to Higher Education," *American Sociological Review*, vol. 75, no. 2, 2010.

63   "A third option . . .": Jeannie Oakes and Marisa Saunders,

eds., *Beyond Tracking: Multiple Pathways to College, Career, and Civic Participation* (Cambridge, MA: Harvard Education Press, 2008).

Chapter 3

78   "... Dewey predicted ...": John Dewey, *Democracy and Education* (New York: Macmillan, 1916; repr. New York: Free Press, 1994).

78   "... it has found full expression ...": John Henry Newman, *The Idea of a University*, ed. with intro and notes by Ian T. Ker (Oxford, UK: Clarendon Press, 1st ed., 1852).

79   "... widely reviewed book ...": Hacker and Dreifus, *Higher Education?*

Chapter 4

84   "... according to one study, only 16 percent ...": Michael Lawrence Collins, "Overview of the National Landscape for Developmental Education Improvement: Testimony Before the State Senate Higher Education Committee" (Washington, DC: Developmental Education Initiative, June 18, 2010), 5.

86   "... in one study, 24 percent ..." Paul Attewell et al., "New Evidence on College Remediation," *Journal of Higher Education*, vol. 77, 2006, 886–924.

87   "On a visit to some college friends ...": This vignette is drawn from my *Lives on the Boundary* (New York: Free Press, 1989).

95   "Early nineteenth-century educators ...": Stanley J. Zehm, "Educational Misfits: A Study of Poor Performers in the English Class, 1825–1925" (Diss., Stanford University, 1973).

96   "Remediation in higher education...": Mike Rose, "The Language of Exclusion: Writing Instruction at the University," *College English*, vol. 47, no. 4, April 1985; Jane Stanley, *The Rhetoric of Remediation* (Pittsburgh, PA: University of Pittsburgh Press, 2010).

102   ". . . 60 percent of new nurses . . .": Arthur Viterito and Carolyn Teich, "Research Brief: The Nursing Shortage and the Role of Community Colleges in Nurse Education" (Washington, DC: American Association of Community Colleges, 2002).

Chapter 5

118   ". . . I tell that story elsewhere . . .": Rose, *Lives on the Boundary*.

119   "Eventually, I and my colleagues . . . further developed the curriculum . . .": Mike Rose and Malcolm Kiniry, *Critical Strategies for Academic Thinking and Writing*, 3rd ed. (Boston: St. Martin's Press, 1998).

122– "The problem is that we have over half-a-century's worth of
123   research . . .": This research is addressed in Mike Rose, *An Open Language: Selected Writing on Literacy, Learning, and Opportunity* (Boston: St. Martin's Press, 2006). The discussion of re-mediation in this chapter draws on the work in my *An Open Language*. See also David Bartholomae, *Writing on the Margins: Essays on Composition and Teaching* (Boston: St. Martin's Press, 2005); W. Norton Grubb and Helena Worthen, *Honored but Invisible: An Inside Look at Teaching in the Community Colleges* (New York: Routledge, 1999); Mary Soliday, *The Politics of Remediation: Institutions and Student Needs in Higher Education* (Pittsburgh, PA: University of Pittsburgh Press, 2002); and Jane Stanley, *The Rhetoric of Remediation: Negotiating Entitlement*

and Access to Higher Education (Pittsburgh, PA: University of Pittsburgh Press, 2010).

125   "One influential expert . . .": Samuel Orton, "The 'Sight Reading' Method of Teaching Reading as a Source of Reading Disability," *Journal of Educational Psychology*, vol. 20, 1929, 135–143.

125   ". . . 1930 textbook on written . . .": Alfred Lang, *Modern Methods in Written Examinations* (Boston: Houghton Mifflin, 1930), 38.

127   "Witness *The Bell* Curve. . .": Richard J. Hernstein and Charles Murray, *The Bell Curve.*

128   "But . . . remedial education has worked for some students . . ." Paul Attewell et al., "New Evidence on College Remediation," *Journal of Higher Education*, vol. 77, 2006, 886–924.

133   "This is the kind of thing that captivated me . . .": Rose, *The Mind at Work.*

133   "In *The Republic* Plato . . .": Plato, *The Republic of Plato,* trans. F.M. Cornford (Oxford, UK: Oxford University Press, 1945), 203.

133   ". . . and in his *Politics* . . .": Aristotle, *Politics, Book 6,* trans. H. Rackham (Cambridge, MA: Harvard University Press, 1972), 503.

134   "Looking back over our history . . .": John P. Hoerr, *And the Wolf Finally Came: The Decline of the American Steel Industry* (Pittsburgh, PA: University of Pittsburgh Press, 1988), 273.

134   "At the postsecondary level, as historian . . .": Laurence Veysey, *The Emergence of the American University* (Chicago: University of Chicago Press, 1965).

137 "But as with remedial education, this is a promising moment.": For some examples of promising instructional work in remediation and vocational education, see Peter Adams et al., "The Accelerated Learning Program: Throwing Open the Gates," *Journal of Basic Writing*, vol. 28, no. 2, 2009, 50–69; Nikki Edgecombe, "Accelerating the Academic Achievement of Students Referred to Developmental Education," Working Paper no. 30 (New York: Community College Research Center, 2011); Katie Hern and Myra Snell, "Exponential Attrition and the Promise of Acceleration in Developmental English and Math," unpublished paper, 2010; Dolores Perin, "Facilitating Student Learning Through Contextualization," Working Paper no. 29 (New York: Community College Research Center, 2011); Charles W. Wiseley, "Effective Basic Skills Instruction: The Case for Contextualized Developmental Math," Policy Brief 10-5 (Stanford, CA: Policy Analysis for California Education, 2011).

139 ". . . you can read the best of research methodologists . . .": Donald T. Campbell, *Methodology and Epistemology for Social Sciences*, ed. E.S. Overman (Chicago: University of Chicago Press, 1988); Lee J. Cronbach, "Beyond the Two Disciplines of Scientific Psychology," *American Psychologist*, vol. 30, 1975, 116–126.

140 "As Bill Gates said . . .'drill in' on that skill.": Marketplace Life, Interview with Bill Gates, February 28, 2011. www.marketplace.org/topics/life/importance-teachers-education.

141 "We have here the makings in education . . . ": Michael B. Katz, *The Undeserving Poor: From the War on Poverty to the War on Welfare* (New York: Pantheon, 1990).

Chapter 6

147   **The Physical Environment:** "This section draws on . . .":
       C. Carney Strange and James H. Banning, *Educating by Design:*
       Creating Campus Learning Environments That Work (San Francisco:
       Jossey-Bass, 2001).

170   ". . . undergraduate curriculum from the 1950s.": Frederick
       Rudolph, *Curriculum: A History of the American Undergraduate*
       Course of Study Since 1636 (San Francisco: Jossey-Bass,
       1978).

173   "The sociologist James Rosenbaum...": James E. Rosenbaum,
       Regina Deil-Amen, and Ann E. Person, *After Admission:*
       From College Access to College Success (New York: Russell Sage
       Foundation, 2006).

Conclusion

184   "As historian Joseph Kett put it . . .": Joseph Kett, *The Pursuit*
       of Knowledge Under Difficulties: From Self-Improvement to Adult
       Education in America, 1750–1990 (Stanford, CA: Stanford
       University Press, 1994).